The Dream Oracle

The Dream Oracle

DAVID F. MELBOURNE
and
DR KEITH HEARNE

NEW HOLLAND

To Liz, who is courageously coping with multiple sclerosis.

First published in 1998 by
New Holland Publishers (UK) Ltd
A member of the New Holland Struik Group of Companies
London • Cape Town • Sydney • Singapore

24 Nutford Place
London W1H 6DQ
United Kingdom

80 McKenzie Street
Cape Town 8001
South Africa

3/2 Aquatic Drive
Frenchs Forest, NSW 2086
Australia

2 4 6 8 10 9 7 5 3

ISBN 1 85368 975 0 (hb)
ISBN 1 85368 976 9 (pb)

Editorial Management: Complete Editions
Editor: Sandy Ransford
Designer: Harold King
Cover Design: Grahame Dudley Associates
Special Photography: Mark Turner
Images of sleeping girl, waves and humming bird: Image Bank

Set in Gill Sans by Pitfold Design, Hindhead, England
Cover reproduction by Dot Gradations
Printed and bound in Singapore by Kyodo Printing Co (Singapore) Pte Ltd

Contents

FOREWORD

For many years I have been dedicated to unravelling the mysteries of dreams. After studying the theories of psychologists, and of Sigmund Freud, Carl Gustav Jung, F. S. Perls and many others, I began to develop my own ideas. Eventually, through reading the results of Keith Hearne's research into dreams, I cracked the secret code of dream meanings. I developed what is now regarded as a proven method of dream interpretation, which I have named the Melbourne cross-reference flow chart system.

Although the flow chart method is relatively simple to use, acquiring the basic knowledge required to operate the system is far from easy. It requires the would-be analyst to cultivate an understanding of all theories, both past and present.

While this is appropriate for the dedicated dreams enthusiast, it becomes a daunting prospect for individuals who wish to know the meaning of dreams, but who, for various reasons, have neither the time nor the inclination to embark on a course of such intensive study.

Through association with the astrologer Helen Adams, which led to the use of astrology in dream interpretation, my method evolved into a holistic system (astro-oneiroscopy) which resulted in dream analysis so finely tuned that the interpretations contained an incredible amount of accurate detail – far beyond what would normally be expected from an analyst. For example, we have evidence to substantiate our claim that astro-oneiroscopy can be used as a healing tool for mind, body and spirit.

Nonetheless, I still found myself speculating about the person who desired to understand the meaning of dreams, but did not have the time or level of commitment necessary to learn the process of decoding them. I knew that such people could be numbered in millions.

For years I have been programming my subconscious to give me a dream to fit my requirements (this centuries-old process is known as "incubating" dreams), yet strangely, I had not consciously incubated a dream to solve the dilemma of how to provide an easy method of interpreting dreams for people with no knowledge of the subject. Nevertheless, the problem had been on my mind for a long time.

As Dr Hearne and I were nearing the completion of a substantial project, I began working on another. It was then, after approximately one month, that I awoke with the idea of an oracular system for dream interpretation. Whilst I was unable to remember any specific dream, the idea for this book was floating around in my head from the moment I opened my eyes. It seems likely, therefore, that I received the inspiration for it from a dream. Indeed, I have become attuned to noting down my impressions upon waking, and have frequently come up with useful concepts as a result. (One wonders exactly how many intriguing discoveries are hovering around in the world of dreams, just waiting to be revealed and remembered.)

For the rest of that day, I found myself unable to concentrate on work. As the idea for *The Dream Oracle* began to take shape, I was barely able to contain my excitement. Finally, after a week or two, I had an outline which, as far as I could see, had no flaws whatsoever. Although *The Dream Oracle* does not provide a detailed interpretation of a specific dream, it will translate the meaning of the theme of the message which is being transmitted from the subconscious to the conscious mind.

For those who wish to establish a detailed interpretation, *The Dream Oracle* can be used in tandem with the two previously mentioned methods, which I have written about in other books (see Bibliography), thus short-circuiting much of the routine investigative work. In other words, the combined system will identify the correct theme immediately. Then a more detailed analysis can be sought using the cross-reference flow chart system. After that, if one requires advice as to how to achieve a better balance in life, the holistic method can be pursued. We hope that, between these three techniques, all aspects of dream interpretation will have been covered – making the meaning of dreams accessible to all.

I had always envisaged writing *The Dream Oracle* in collaboration with Keith Hearne – there were advantages attached to making it a joint project. He is an internationally renowned psychologist, who is skilled in many aspects of science. In addition, I had long since regarded him as the world's leading authority on the subject of dreams. If anybody could find a flaw in *The Dream Oracle*, it would be him. Moreover, during our professional association, we had become close friends and I soon learned how adept he is at explaining the theory behind an idea and finding flaws, if any. At the very least, I needed to explain to him the principles of *The Dream Oracle*, then monitor his reaction.

During the next couple of days we decided on the structure for the book, and a week later, we began writing. It was during this process that *The Dream Oracle* taught me that there are other rewards to be had through its use. An instance of this is a story of what led to my first "O" dream.

I had written the *Oracle* up to and including the letter "V" when I discovered that another major project on which I had previously worked required a considerable amount of rewriting, so it would be better suited for the intended market. I dropped what I was doing and gave the rewrite priority over everything. In fact, I burned the midnight oil solidly for a fortnight to get the job done – I didn't rest until it was completed. I suffer from a recurring eye disease, and the task had activated it slightly, causing mild inflammation.

As if on cue, the night I finished the work, *The Dream Oracle* decided to prove how efficiently it worked. I dreamed that Dr Hearne approached me with an additional chapter for another book. He held out some paper on which a huge letter "O" was printed in bold type. For a fraction of a second, I realized that I was dreaming – in other words, I became lucid – which later enabled me to remember the dream in detail.

The following morning, I read my own words about the meaning of such a dream. According to the *Oracle*, "O" stands for "overuse". The moment I scanned the passage about eye strain, I knew instinctively that my subconscious had used this example to prove exactly how it can home in on an issue with pin-point accuracy. The instant I told Keith Hearne of my dream, he asked if I had become lucid. It dawned on me that I had, albeit for a fraction of a second. Then the realization hit me. I knew that *The Dream Oracle* was signalling something else. Really, it was screaming at me, "This system can also be used to induce a lucid dream!"

Soon after this, it struck me that I had achieved a lifetime's ambition. Since the beginning of dream research, nobody has been able to prove that dreams actually bear messages. Until now, it has been a matter of speculation and conjecture, although I've always believed that this was one of the purposes of dreams. *The Dream Oracle* proves beyond doubt that some dreams do bring us messages directly from the subconscious. For the first time, without the use of drugs or hypnosis, *The Dream Oracle* enables us to set up an avenue of communication from the subconscious directly to the conscious mind. At last, the subconscious can share its seemingly infinite store of wisdom with us!

Finally, having analyzed literally thousands of dreams, it occurred to me that accurate interpretations sometimes alert dreamers to on-going problems of which they have been unaware – this often involves some sort of duplicity by third parties.

As you read *The Dream Oracle*, you will encounter passages that point out that if a clear message does not become apparent, you should give the matter a lot of thought – after which, an answer should be forthcoming. We say this to encourage you to look deeper into your thoughts about the matter to be resolved, especially where it may involve a third party.

Good luck and happy dreaming!

David F. Melbourne

INTRODUCTION

The fact that dream symbols are personal to each and every individual has made the subject of dream interpretation uncertain and often difficult. *The Dream Oracle* provides a revolutionary new method whereby our unconscious is given a standard set of meanings in the form of an alphabetical list to be read before we go to sleep. This very simple new system enables our unconscious mind to give a wise answer to a significant question by identifying dreams containing subjects whose names begin with a specific letter. The relevant letter may appear directly within a dream, or may be strongly indicated by a sequence of items appearing beginning with the appropriate letter (e.g. a dream sequence involving potatoes, police, paper, etc., which emphasize the letter "P", which according to the *Oracle* represents patience). On waking, the initial letters of the subjects most commonly seen in the dream are noted down and the one which recurs most often is consulted in The Standard, Universal, Alphabetic Dream Code (pp 85-166) in order to comprehend the full meaning of the dream.

Our unconscious is really a vast information bank containing information about our physical and psychological condition now, in the past and as currently projected into the future. It also has a deep knowledge of everything that we have ever experienced, whether consciously or subliminally. For example, someone may have said one thing to us, but our unconscious may have picked up different, non-verbal signals or messages. Therein lies the wisdom of the unconscious, which will have registered discrepancies and, if asked, will articulate them in response to a dream. The paranormal element in dreams has been well documented. This relates particularly to premonition dreams.

The new *Dream Oracle* method also facilitates the communication of such psychic information. Dreams have been used as an oracle for millenia. But in the past, their interpretation has only been dealt with by experts. The new method makes the requested answer to a question about the meaning of a dream very specific and easy to understand by anybody – without the need for complicated decoding.

There are moments when significant leaps are made in mankind's progress towards greater self-insight. David Melbourne has made such an advance by his notion of *The Dream Oracle.*

Startlingly simple in concept, as good ideas are, it is a method of obtaining important specific guidance from our unconscious using the vehicle of the dream. Although David is a dream interpreter, his revolutionary new technique for understanding the messages contained in our dreams does not actually require interpretational skills.

There is much evidence that the unconscious possesses considerable, detailed information about an individual. Work in Past Life Regression indicates that even information about previous lives is also held in store and that emotional, mental, physical and spiritual residues from those lives may still exert an influence on the current existence.

Often, what we call "the caring unconscious" is fully aware of situations of which the conscious mind is completely unaware. However, there is a major problem of communication between them. Sometimes the attitude of the unconscious, in protecting the individual, will, for instance, cause a psychosomatic illness to develop in order to avoid a potentially difficult or dangerous situation, or the individual's real but not yet conscious opinion about an issue may emerge vocally as an inadvertent slip of the tongue. Or the unconscious may communicate bodily, through physical pain – a migraine, say, or some other physical sensation. In conversion reaction neurotics, the unconscious thought of feeling trapped in a situation will be reflected directly as physical paralysis.

Unconscious thoughts are also represented in dreams, not necessarily as heavily disguised wishes, but simply because the dream's language is visual and symbolic.

It is difficult, however, for people to interpret their dreams accurately and gain insight from the knowledge that is portrayed in them. Dream dictionaries, which give standard or universal meanings, are not useful in reality, since there are vast individual differences in symbolic imagery.

David Melbourne's great contribution has been to provide a

simple, standard, universal dream-code language that the unconscious can use to communicate its attitude and opinion to the dreamer's conscious mind. Dream interpretation in itself is avoided, therefore, but a specific, meaningful and unambiguous message can be conveyed easily to our consciousness.

The Dream Oracle provides the unconscious with a fixed list of possible answers to a question posed to it by an individual. In response, their unconscious will be able to reveal its knowledge by reflecting one of the pre-stated store of answers in the dream. By-passing the necessity for dream interpretation, each possible answer is linked to a letter of the alphabet. The selected letter will be made obvious in a direct or indirect way, and hence reveal the appropriate answer. David Melbourne and I believe that the inevitable consequence of this discovery is that a new, universal language of specific, alphabet-related answers will become established in popular usage and enter the group consciousness. Thus, if someone mentions having experienced a "J" dream, people will know that the answer refers specifically to the topic of Joy, or if they have an "E" dream, the answer will be on the theme of Envy, and so on, according to the dream code contained in the *Oracle*.

This discovery represents a really significant advance in conventional dream psychology, and its second, metaphysical, function is as significant, or more so, than the ancient Chinese invention of the *I Ching*.

HOW TO USE *THE DREAM ORACLE* TO OBTAIN MESSAGE-BEARING DREAMS

Firstly, the user should focus on a personal issue that is unresolved. For a comment on a major topic, the significance of the matter can be impressed upon the unconscious by ritualistic cleansing and, if medically safe, perhaps fasting for a whole day or even longer, prior to sleep and dreaming. These are well established "dream-incubation" techniques (see pages 41 to 42 and 82 to 84), which encourage the unconscious to respond in a clear way through dreams.

Before going to sleep, the subject then establishes a database for their unconscious which will apply to any issue which they wish to resolve. To do this, they read the fixed range of 26 possible answer-themes which are given in *The Dream Oracle*. Each answer-theme is linked to a letter of the alphabet, and is further subdivided into specific answers, all of which will register firmly in the unconscious mind of the dreamer. This is what we call the Standard, Universal, Alphabetic Dream Code.

Thirdly, following the dream, or upon waking up, the subject should write down a report of their dream. A letter of the alphabet may have been seen in the dream, or several major items beginning with the same letter may have been identified in the dream. By writing down the content of the dream, the significant letter of the alphabet may be easily singled out.

Lastly, the user again consults the list of possible responses in *The Dream Oracle* and is reminded consciously of the corresponding answer to the selected alphabetical letter. The letter gives the theme of the answer and the particular answer in the list under that theme will be obvious to the user.

The result is a meaningful message from the user's unconscious, uninfluenced by conscious biases: the unconsciously chosen answer is immediately obtained by consulting the fixed list of responses.

The potential of the method was demonstrated early on when it was being devised. David, Helen Adams, the astrologer, and I were the first three people to read the list of dream-code themes, and each of us soon experienced a message-bearing dream using the new method.

David reports his first alphabetic-code dream in the Foreword of this book. Another interesting one that happened to him was a dream in which he saw the letter "R". It concerned repentance, and he realized he had made an error of judgement about someone, and his unconscious was urgently telling him to think again. The message instantly changed his attitude about the person.

A few nights after seeing the standard alphabetical meanings, Helen had a vivid dream of seeing the letter "F". Her unconscious instantly woke her up, here too reinforcing the significance of the message (the trigger effect). "F" stands for faith. The specific answer in the theme's list that stood out for her concerned having and maintaining faith in her plans. It was absolutely appropriate to her current state of mind and it gave her new determination. Since then, many other cases have confirmed the usefulness of the new process.

My own first case occurred when I pinned up the alphabetic code list by my bed. That night I experienced many dreams in which very many objects beginning with the letter "B" appeared – bus, bridge, baby, balloon, and so on. The message, concerning brevity, contained clear guidance for me at that particular time.

We anticipate that *The Dream Oracle* will be widely employed as a psychological tool by therapists and psychiatrists. It will provide important truths concerning the client/patient, and short-cut the processes of understanding and healing.

Also, increasing numbers of people are seeking a greater spirituality through self-insight and awareness. *The Dream Oracle* is an ideal pathway for gaining that self-knowledge. It can save years of truth-seeking through conventional means.

Evidence overwhelmingly suggests that the unconscious can receive telepathic, clairvoyant and precognitive information. Another use of the technique is to call on the supernormal powers of the unconscious in order that we may gain access to certain distant information. This is the second, oracular function of the process.

Official science cannot, at the moment, countenance such notions, but ordinary people already know that paranormal events happen. The age-old concepts of the paranormal had necessarily to be embodied in *The Dream Oracle* because they are part of the real world.

A word of warning. There seem to be powerful laws of balance in the cosmos, and it is recognized that oracles should not be over-used. Therefore *The Dream Oracle*, when used as an oracle rather than as a method for receiving messages from the unconscious about yourself, should be used sparingly. It should certainly not be used for financial or material gain, and it must be regarded as an aid to higher spirituality. To guard against abuse, *The Dream Oracle* has its own in-built indicator under the letter "O" – for overuse.

There can only be one version of *The Dream Oracle*. Its language, with which people will become familiar, will become universal and part of common knowledge, just as the tarot symbols and meanings are recognized and understood throughout the world.

Let us use *The Dream Oracle* to advance from materialistic illusions and find freedom through seeking the truth.

Dr Keith Hearne

Part One

CHAPTER 1

The Power of the Unconscious

What is the evidence that we all possess a knowledgeable yet "submerged" or "unconscious" component to our minds – and to what extent can it influence us? Before Sigmund Freud drew particular attention to the unconscious, its existence was postulated as the "hidden self" by William James and as the "subliminal self" by F. W. H. Myers. Freud pointed out that there were unconscious and pre-conscious parts to our minds, which contain information that could potentially become conscious, as, for example, with a temporarily forgotten name.

In simple terms, Freud conceptualized the personality as having a tri-partite structure: the primitive Id, which seeks gratification of basic, instinctual desires, especially sex; the Ego, the conscious item in contact with the real world; and the Super-ego, which encapsulates how the individual ought to behave in society.

The Ego is somewhat uncomfortably positioned between the incessant and unreasonable desires of the Id and the tut-tutting reminders of the Super-ego. It constantly attempts to appease both sides.

Freud considered that much of the mind operates at an unconscious level, and that the real (and, perhaps, consciously unacceptable) reasons for our superficially altruistic behaviour may be found there. He believed that the dream in particular could reveal the workings of the unconscious. "The dream," he declared, "is the *via regis* (royal road) to a knowledge of the unconscious."

The purpose of Freudian, psycho-analytical therapy was to make the unconscious conscious, in order to obtain greater self-understanding.

OUR NATURAL DEFENCES

Sometimes, situations in our lives can cause overwhelming conflicts and, to protect the Ego, various defence mechanisms may come into play. For example, a person may deny that an event ever happened, or some disturbing memory may be actively repressed. Our own unacceptable impulses, such as aggression, may be projected on to someone else so that we perceive that person, wrongly, as menacing. Or we may displace an unpalatable thought elsewhere, so that the Oedipal impulse about one's mother is generalized towards women having her features. We may earnestly believe the opposite of what is true. A feeling of aggression towards a child may be hidden from the Ego by an over-protective attitude towards that child. Good reasons may be given for something, which are not really true. Thus, a man's desire to molest a woman may be excused by thinking that she in some way "deserves it".

PERCEPTUAL DEFENCE

Psychological experiments have shown that emotionally disturbing words are more difficult to recognize than neutral words, a finding we would expect if defence mechanisms do actually operate. This phenomenon is generally known as "perceptual defence".

Extensive work, especially by British researcher Norman Dixon, has given clear support for the Freudian notion of defence. In a typical experiment using a "closed loop" method, subjects were shown, to one eye, emotive words such as "cancer" and "breast", and neutral words such as "recant" and "stance", all equal in size, brightness, and so on. They were subliminal and could not be seen consciously. Spots of light were projected into the other eye and the subject could vary their brightness, with the intention of having one light just visible and the other invisible. The perceptual threshold increased (i.e. subjects increased the brightness control) when the emotive words were being perceived by the unconscious.

CONVERSION REACTIONS

Clinically, one of the clearest and most dramatic links between the unconscious mind and the body is illustrated in the condition known as "conversion reaction neurosis", where a psychological conflict is converted to an actual physical disorder. The unconscious is aware of the deception, yet the conscious mind is fooled.

One young woman, aged 16, was admitted to hospital with apparent bodily paralysis which did not correspond with the nervous system's layout. It was a hysterical or false paralysis of psychological cause, and it gradually improved, though it later internalized and affected her colon. It was only after some 30 years that she saw the link between the bodily paralysis and her gut problem, which then began to improve.

This same woman exhibits frequent bodily indicators of her psychological state. If she "doesn't wish to see something", she develops eyesight problems. If she has "something on her mind", she develops a migraine. Recently she was working on a help-line and described how, as one customer was becoming unreasonably obnoxious, she found herself developing increasing deafness. She is a walking physical barometer of her current psychological state and is an unusual example of how unconscious thoughts and attitudes can directly affect the body.

THE UNCONSCIOUS IN EVERYDAY LIFE

The operation of unconscious drives may be observed in a number of everyday life situations. In jokes, according to Freud, the effect of unconscious factors may emerge. The joke can evade the censorious Super-ego and a personal truth may be touched upon, the excessive laughter reflecting the strength of repressed feeling involved. Wit, especially the barbed variety, is considered to be motivated by aggression and neuroticism, whereas jokes are a healthy coping mechanism.

Defences sometimes fail and the real, unconscious attitude can spill out, such as when we make slips of the tongue. A person inadvertently saying, "Shut the bore," instead of, "Shut the door," may be exposing their true attitude towards someone whom they find dull.

Such indications of unresolved conflicts are more likely to occur in stressful situations. Our own slips of the tongue can be useful to us in communicating the presence of doubt or problems about the topic or person we are discussing.

The evidence so far points to the existence of a discrete part of the mind that is separate from consciousness and which – in a sense – "fools" the conscious part by preventing certain truths from reaching insightful awareness.

In order for defences to work, there has to be a part of the mind that knows which areas are vulnerable – what the limits of self-awareness are. This defensive part has a "mind of its own", yet is completely inaccessible to waking consciousness. It is called the unconscious.

THE JUNGIAN UNCONSCIOUS

The Jungian understanding of the unconscious is perhaps more far-reaching, and sees it as a much more amiable component of the individual. It is a friend, guide and adviser, and has a perspective that includes future planning. Jung asserted that apart from our own personal unconscious, there also exists a collective unconscious to which we are all linked.

Therapists come across examples of the guiding, caring unconscious frequently, and it is an aspect that is called upon for assistance in *The Dream Oracle* technique.

Freud was rather uncompromising about the sexual basis of dreams, but Jung saw a wider perspective. Inserting a key into a lock, seen in a dream, might be a sexual symbol, or it might simply symbolize a metaphorical desire to open new doors in one's life. The significance of the key symbol is always specific to the individual.

Jung saw the dream as giving important messages which helped to balance the individual's psyche. He tells of one man who developed a passion for mountain climbing. In a dream, the man saw himself stepping off into space. Jung was concerned and tried to make him see that it was a dire warning of death in a mountain accident. The man took no notice and six months later fell to his death, knocking his friend to his death also.

Jung also recognized that developing illness and disease can be portrayed by the unconscious in dreams long before the symptoms become noticeable consciously.

CREATIVITY AND THE UNCONSCIOUS

The truly vast potential of the unconscious is exemplified by the number of remarkable works in the arts and sciences that have originated in the form of dreams. We often consider problems are worth "sleeping on", so that a considered answer is arrived at by automatic, intelligent, inner processes.

The creative advantage of the dream state may be due to the fact that unusual and unexpected links are made between ideas by the unconscious, links that would tend not to occur in consciousness because of various biases.

THE PARANORMAL AND THE UNCONSCIOUS

Another demonstration of the power of the unconscious is perhaps the facilitating effect that seems to happen in, say, dream-telepathy experiments. A fascinating series of experiments was conducted at Maimonides Hospital in New

York in the 1960s, when Ullman and Krippner produced evidence of telepathy happening in the dream state.

Typically, the "receiver" was wired up in the sleep laboratory and woken to give dream reports after monitored REM periods. The "transmitter" person concentrated and attempted to project a randomly selected theme into the receiver's dreams. This procedure was repeated over several nights, using different target material each night.

Later, the dream subject and "naive" judges rated the degree of similarity between each night's dreams and each set of possible target material (including the actual one). Statistical tests then determined the likelihood of telepathy having been involved. Several of the studies gave *highly* significant results, suggesting that telepathy was operating in the dream state.

THE UNCONSCIOUS IN THERAPY

Material which has remained submerged in the unconscious for many years can suddenly surface, sometimes dramatically, in therapy sessions. For instance, a woman was hypnotically regressed to childhood and started gagging. Told to move outside her body and observe the events, she described how a neighbour at that time was making her perform oral sex on him. She remembered the unpleasant smell of him and how the events happened behind a door. Many suppressed details came back to her. It was a significant first step in her therapy.

PAST LIFE THERAPY

Some of the most amazing material presented in therapy appears to come from unconscious past life memories of the individual. Thus, a woman in her forties who was regressed to a time in this life when she had an abortion, began to sob bitterly. Instantly, she found herself in a temple in very ancient times. She was a priestess, but had given birth, and the baby was being taken away. She cradled it lovingly in her arms, still crying. Then a great insight overcame her. "It's the same baby!" she exclaimed incredulously. It was the same spirit of the baby she had aborted in this lifetime. She then realized that the spirit had eventually reached her, because her daughter was born years after the abortion. She felt a particular closeness to her daughter, which the session explained to her.

THE UNCONSCIOUS STATE

From a variety of approaches, there is much evidence of an advanced state of awareness and organization that is normally unavailable to consciousness, i.e. it is unconscious.

At an experimental, scientific level, studies in perceptual defence give clear backing that the notion, and clinically, the condition, where a psychological conflict is unwittingly represented in a physical disability (this is known as a conversion reaction), is a clear manifestation of "another state" of organization of the individual.

There are indications of unconscious workings in things we come across every day – mistakes in behaviour that imply a different attitude from that stated openly. Further implications are revealed by creative processes and paranormal phenomena.

In psychology, the unconscious has been accepted, as central to their theories, by Freud and Jung, and manifestations of unconscious effects are observed frequently by therapists.

CHAPTER 2

Ancient Dream Knowledge

It has long been known that dreams harbour a very considerable wisdom. The ancients noticed that dreams could, say, come up with a cure for an individual's illness, or provide a timely warning of some kind to the dreamer – perhaps of disloyalty by someone close, or of impending disaster such as a severe illness.

In addition, some extra information seemed to be what we would now call paranormal, arriving by routes that did not involve the known sensory systems. It was as if some super-aware entity – a god – possessed special information about the person and their life circumstances. Certainly, to people in ancient times, dreams could be expected to provide information that was advantageous to the dreamer.

There is a tendency in many scientists nowadays to patronize the findings of those early peoples, but we should not be so arrogant as to think that the ancients were any less intelligent than modern humankind. The evidence is that people in early societies were extremely good at observing different phenomena and noticing any meaningful connections.

They were natural scientists and pragmatically used the knowledge they acquired for practical use. They learned about the medicinal powers of different plants, techniques of farming and agriculture, and the movement of the stars in the sky.

Consider the vast knowledge that was involved in the building of the pyramids of ancient Egypt. The builders' mathematical and constructional skills were considerable and the pyramids' orientation to certain stars was precise.

The ancient Greeks knew much about our solar system from simple observation, without complex instrumentation. Over 200 years before Christ, Eratosthenes used trigonometry to calculate the circumference of the earth. His method involved measuring shadow lengths at two different locations on a north-south line at the highest point of the sun on midsummer's day.

In about the same period, Aristarchus worked out the distance to the moon. He also suggested that the sun is at the centre of the solar system – a view that went unrecognized until Copernicus came to the same conclusion some 1800 years later.

It is only sensible, then, to give due regard to other areas of interest to the ancients – in particular, with reference to this book, the topic of the dream.

The ancients had accumulated much knowledge about dreams by straightforward and careful observation. Unencumbered by dubious modern psychological "theories", their approach was purely practical and based on much experience.

ANCIENT ASSYRIA AND BABYLONIA

The great library at Nineveh (5000 BC) housed cuneiform-script clay tablets recording Assyrian and Babylonian knowledge of dream meanings. There was obviously an understanding then that dreams could be decoded. In Babylonia, temples existed to the dream goddess Mamu. Various rituals were conducted in these temples to abolish unpleasant dreams and to encourage meaningful dreams.

ANCIENT EGYPT

The ancient Egyptians held the belief that dreams *(omina)* were messages from the gods. The Chester Beatty papyrus (1350 BC) gives much insight into their ideas on dreams.

One ancient dream document, published in the 18th dynasty (1500 BC) provided a list of dream behaviour with comments as to its meaning. Some were favourable omens and some indicated that trouble lay ahead, for instance, if a woman dreamed of kissing her husband. This example incorporates the universally observed notion of "opposites", that the dream activity may sometimes represent the contrary to what it appears to foretell.

An interesting inscription on the Sphinx at Giza records a precognitive dream of Thutmose III (1450 BC) in which he was promised the kingdom if he cleared the then extensive obscuration of the Sphinx by sand.

ANCIENT CHINA

In ancient Chinese society, dreams were thought to be caused by the spiritual soul, or *hun*, travelling about during sleep. Dream interpretation in that culture included astrological factors. If the energy systems of Yin and Yang were out of balance, distressing dreams would result. The *Lie-tseu,* a Taoist document, catalogued six different types of dream: ordinary dreams, terror dreams, day-residue dreams, dreams of waking, joyful dreams, and dreams of fear.

The "contrary phenomenon" was recognized in this work too, so that a dream of laughing could represent imminent unhappiness. They believed that to understand the dream was therapeutic.

There are two well-known philosophical comments concerning dreams by the great 4th-century BC sage Chuang-tzu, who challenged our notion of reality:

> While men are dreaming, they do not perceive that it is a dream. Some will even have a dream in a dream and only when they wake they know it was a dream. And so, when the Great

Awakening comes upon us, shall we know this life to be a great dream. Fools believe themselves to be awake now.

Once upon a time, I, Chuang-tzu, dreamed I was a butterfly fluttering hither and thither, to all intents and purposes a butterfly. I was conscious only of following my fancies as a butterfly, and was unaware of my individuality as a butterfly. Suddenly I was awakened and there I lay myself again. Now I do not know whether I was a man dreaming I was a butterfly, or whether I am a butterfly dreaming I am a man.

ANCIENT GREECE

The Greeks believed the gods could communicate with humans via Hypnos, the god of sleep, and Morpheus, the god of dreams. Dreams were the result of such nocturnal visitations.

True and false dreams were recognized. Homer, author of *The Iliad* and *The Odyssey*, stated that true dreams came through the gate of horn; false dreams via the gate of ivory (based on a Greek pun). The ancient Greek physician Hippocrates noticed symbolism in dreams and thought that the universe (macrocosm) might represent the body (microcosm) – so that a shining star could indicate a healthy physical state in the dreamer.

The great Greek philosopher Plato, in his *Republic*, stated that "in all of us, even in good men, there is a lawless wild beast nature which peers out in sleep".

In both Greek and Roman societies, precognitive dreams were regarded seriously. According to Plutarch, another of the great Greek philosophers, Calpurnia, the wife of Julius Caesar, is supposed to have dreamed of his assassination the night before it happened.

Artemidorus of Daldis was a 2nd-century Greek who moved to Rome. He compiled a vast five-volume work on dream interpretation entitled *Oneirocritica*. Artemidorus was familiar with many symbols, including sexual symbolism (e.g. sowing and tilling), and with the concept of opposites in dreams.

ANCIENT INDIA

A treatise on dreams in the *Atharva Veda* (a book of wisdom, 1500 – 1000 BC) states early Indian beliefs concerning dream interpretation. An active, aggressive role in the dream was considered to be more favourable than a passive role.

On the matter of premonitions in dreams, the early Indians held the view that the nearer to waking in the morning the dream occurred, the sooner the event would come to fruition.

They considered a kind of refinement process occurred in dreams during the night, so the later dreams were the best to be interpreted. They also took the dreamer's temperament into account in the overall interpretation.

BIBLICAL DREAMS IN CHRISTIANITY AND ISLAM

Early Biblical dreams were certainly treated as revelations from the divine and actually influenced the course of history. Perhaps the most well-known dream is that of the pharaoh in the Book of Genesis, which Joseph interpreted following a recommendation about his skills from the pharaoh's servant. The pharaoh dreamed of seven fat cattle and seven thin ones, which ate the fat cattle. Joseph saw this as a precognitive dream which foretold seven years of good harvest to be followed by seven years of famine. The pharaoh acted on the dream to build up stores of grain and saved the country.

In the New Testament, Mary's husband Joseph received four important dreams which encouraged him to accept Mary's pregnancy, to escape from Egypt, to return, after a dream informed him of Herod's death, and to settle in Galilee. Joseph clearly accepted the messages as being significant and he obeyed them fully.

Various early Christian writers commented on dreams before the Middle Ages, when the church linked dream divination with sorcery. Gregory of Nyssa (c. 400) thought that dreams revealed the individual's nature and the great driving force of sexual reproduction.

St Augustine (354-430) thought that demons could influence dreams. A prayer attributed to him calls on God to protect him from dreams which "owing to animal images" would result in "pollution".

Much of the Koran is said to have been delivered to Muhammad in his dreams by the angel Gabriel. The famous call to prayers, the *adhan*, given by a muezzin from the mosque's minaret, was taken up as part of the religious ritual as a result of a dream of one of his followers.

The ancient peoples had considerable knowledge about natural things and we have perhaps under-rated their achievements. There is overwhelming evidence that by much careful and intelligent observation over a long period, they knew much about dreams. The dream was regarded by those people in awe as a vehicle for receiving useful information about themselves and their situation in life. They thought of the source of that information as being the gods, whereas nowadays we would suggest that the unconscious provided much of the knowledge conveyed.

As we have seen, dreams have not only helped individuals, some have been immensely important in the development of political and religious structures in the world. Dreams are useful, and that fact has been known since early times.

CHAPTER 3

Dream Incubation and Psychological Expectation

One of the great innovations concerning the receipt of particularly significant messages from dreams was the invention of dream incubation. It may have originated in ancient Assyria and Babylonia and was certainly practised widely in ancient Egypt, where the god of dreams was called Serapis. Dream temples, *serapeums,* were built, in which people slept in order to receive major dream advice – conceptualized in those days as originating from the gods.

Essentially, the incubant would go through a set of rituals designed to establish a powerful mind-set that would encourage the unconscious to respond with a particularly relevant and focused piece of information. It seems that a stand-in could sometimes undergo the dream incubation on behalf of another.

The individual would firstly undergo a prolonged period, perhaps over several days, of fasting, abstaining from sex, cleansing, purifying, making offerings to the gods, and praying.

They may also have taken dream-inducing substances. They might sleep on the skins of animals which had been sacrificed for the purpose, sometimes surrounded by harmless snakes. With such an array of unusual stimuli to concentrate the mind, it is not surprising that significant dreams ensued. It was, by all accounts, a very successful procedure for inducing communication from the unconscious. Indeed, many miraculous cures were reported as a result of dreamed remedies.

Major dream temples existed at Thebes and Memphis in Egypt. After the incubant had reported the dream experiences of the night, these were interpreted by the oracles, called "The Learned Men of the Magic Library".

A famous Greek sleep temple, dedicated to Asclepius, the god of medicine, stood at Epidaurus in Greece. Physician-priests, *therapeutais*, were the intermediaries who interpreted the reported dreams of their patients. At that time when medicine was in its infancy, many incubants attempted to seek cures for their illnesses.

THE UNCONSCIOUS AND HEALING

The unconscious is often aware of the best way to heal the body. In one instance, a light-skinned woman had dark areas of skin under her eyes. She had been treated for a severe thyroid condition and her medication had left unsightly residues under her skin which she found distressing.

She felt a strong urge to go to a sunny place and spend an unusually long time in the sun, against her rational judgement. It was unusual behaviour for her. Her skin peeled, and the revealed deposits simply wiped away. The woman returned from her holiday looking and feeling a decade younger.

It is not inconceivable that her unconscious guided her to the sun and over-exposure, deliberately, in order to heal her.

At some deep level, our unconscious knows how to bring about a natural physical cure.

PRODROMIC DREAMS AND OTHER UNCONSCIOUS INFORMATION

Further indication of the special knowledge possessed by the unconscious about the individual's physical state is revealed in prodromic ("before running") dreams. The person begins to have dreams which symbolically suggest illness which is not yet noticed at a conscious level. Thus, a developing problem with the lungs may be represented by dreams of being in a fire, or a worsening vascular condition may be shown by dreams of restricted water flow.

Such privileged information about the dreamer's body, noticed in prodromic dreams, can reasonably be considered to exist in other areas, concerning mental, emotional and spiritual matters of the individual.

The unconscious, with so much information to hand that has not entered consciousness, is in a position to give insightful, guiding, protective advice on attitudes, real feelings about someone or something, and one's progress through life.

The unconscious will be cognizant, say, of inconsistencies in people that might indicate untrustworthiness, or of a special liking for one person by another.

Many cases have been reported where individuals have had "vocational" dreams which pointed them to certain areas of work in which they then found complete fulfilment.

Another concept, now appearing more acceptable to science, is that a group, collective, consciousness could exist, so that the data base is potentially far more extensive than that of the individual. If other paranormal effects are also accessible, then the wise unconscious definitely needs to be heeded.

The unconscious, then, has a wealth of useful and perhaps crucial information which can potentially be tapped. The new *Dream Oracle* method provides a valid help-line from the unconscious which can assist people in their journey through life.

THE COMMUNICATION PROBLEM

The unconscious cannot communicate easily with consciousness. In extreme cases, when being protective, it might cause a person to have a minor accident in order to avoid a situation which it considers non-beneficial to the individual. Its viewpoint may also, as we saw in Chapter 1, be revealed by slips of the tongue and the like.

The dream is its best channel of communication, but the dream-producing process has various inherent limitations and so alters and distorts the underlying unconscious thoughts. The dream tends to progress along associative pathways and represents things in visual and verbal puns. The message can be decoded by experienced and skilful interpretation, but there is often a degree of uncertainty about the results.

The new advance of *The Dream Oracle*, explained fully in Chapter 6, is that any one of a range of specific messages can be pin-pointed and communicated to consciousness directly.

IMAGINATION, VISUALIZATION AND EXPECTATION

Because we possess imagination and can vividly conjure up almost any scenario and experience any associated emotions, we can relive things that have happened to us, or anticipate events that are due to occur.

People with vivid powers of visualization are particularly able to achieve this, and because of the powerful mind/body (psychosomatic) link, thoughts and ideas can greatly affect the body.

Imagination establishes expectation. We can imagine going to the dentist for a cavity-filling, and we have an expectation of some discomfort. Or we take an aspirin tablet for a pain and have an expectation of relief.

Expectation is central to dream incubation. There is a strong requirement, a demand, even, on the unconscious to provide relevant information. It motivates the unconscious to produce a response.

In dreams, of course, any image may be generated and it will be greatly influenced by any pre-sleep expectation.

Dr Keith Hearne, who spent several years running a sleep-laboratory, reports that he observed many cases of psychological expectation in that situation. One experiment, on memory consolidation in sleep, involved subjects being woken in the night to recite various lists that they had learnt. Many of the subjects, knowing that they were to be disturbed, reported that they had already dreamed of being asked to recall the memorized material.

The expectation phenomenon was most amazingly demonstrated in a sleep-lab study involving the induction in subjects of "lucid" dreams – those in which you actually become aware of being in a dream and can then control the dream events.

Dr Hearne had discovered that electrical pulses given to the wrist in REM (dreaming) sleep were often incorporated into the on-going dream and the anomaly triggered the awareness of dreaming. It was the basis of his "dream machine" invention.

In a "control" study, some subjects were told to expect the pulses when dreaming – but in fact no pulses were administered. This was deliberate, to ascertain the extent of anticipation. Incredibly, some subjects woke up and declared that they had felt the pulses, immediately became lucid, and enjoyed the interesting experience of being conscious in a dream!

Hearne utilized the expectation effect in an experimental technique for inducing lucid dreams, without a dream machine. The method, called FAST (False Awakening with State Testing), relies on an expectation of being disturbed in sleep and a religiously carried out routine, performed on seemingly waking, of detecting whether one is really asleep or awake.

An assistant enters the bedroom, potters around, and then goes out again, at intervals after 6 a.m., when there is more abundant REM sleep. Each time the subject thinks he or she is being disturbed and woken, they automatically carry out certain "state" tests, e.g. switch on the bedside lamp, attempt to float, and so on.

There is a condition called a false awakening in which you dream that you are awake. Everything seems perfectly real about your bedroom until, say, you draw the curtains and it's not your street! The verisimilitude can be so great that subjects often say, "I didn't bother to test, because I knew I was awake," when, in fact, they were asleep.

The rationale behind the FAST technique is that sooner or later, the subject will, because of an expectation effect, *dream* that the assistant has entered the room and then recognize the situation as being a dream.

PLACEBOS

Expectation is behind the well-documented medical phenomenon of the placebo. This is an inert substance given to a patient which has an effect (sometimes dramatic) because the patient *believes* that there will be a certain effect. The degree of expectation is enhanced if the drug is administered in a medical setting by a doctor.

Thus, an injection of saline solution may well cause the rapid onset of sleep in a patient told by a credible person speaking with apparent authority, "This will make you sleep, now."

The placebo effect also enhances the power of some drugs. Often, effects are reported before the substance could realistically have been absorbed into the body.

There are even stories of mentally ill people having been given ECT (electro-convulsive therapy) treatment with devices that were found later not to have been functioning, yet with apparent good results.

Expectation has been described here because the unconscious usually has to be primed, in order to precipitate significant information. The ancients knew this, and increased expectation by using rituals.

THE IMPORTANCE OF RITUAL

Ceremonial rituals establish firm memory markers that give the imprint of significance on behaviour. The conscious and unconscious mind take note of the events and give them priority status. Weddings, funerals, graduations, celebration parties and the like emphasize the meaningfulness of the occasion.

The importance of ritual is well known to therapists. If there has not been a "proper" ending to a situation, the psychological wound may not heal. In another scenario, a simple statement asking for forgiveness or giving forgiveness has immense therapeutic worth.

In the procedure of dream incubation, the unconscious will pay more attention to the request for information in the form of a dream if the request is accompanied by unusual ritual.

THE ROLE OF DREAM INCUBATION

To sum up, the role of dream incubation, since ancient times, has been a successful technique for obtaining guidance and advice for individuals. Ritual became a necessary part of the incubation procedure, designed to establish a high expectation of such communication. Expectation is, of course, a significant factor in the placebo effect in medicine.

The nature of the relayed information, which had to be decoded by skilled interpreters, was such that it could advise on many topics of interest to the incubant, including health, relationships and business.

The unconscious possesses much data which could potentially be of great use to the person if it could be accessed. And the data base may extend beyond the individual's personal experience and include collective unconscious information and possibly even that received by paranormal means.

This essential problem of a lack of direct communication from the unconscious to the conscious mind is overcome in *The Dream Oracle* technique.

CHAPTER 4

Recent Dream Knowledge

*T*he *Dream Oracle* involves using the dream state to establish a channel of communication from the unconscious. Let's look at this fascinating area of sleep and dreams to help our understanding of what happens to us during sleep, of the nature of dreams, and of the different phenomena that we might encounter.

TYPES OF SLEEP

*S*leep is composed of two distinct states, termed Slow Wave Sleep (SWS) and Rapid Eye Movement (REM) sleep. SWS is so called because, in the sleep laboratory, people in that state exhibit large, slow brain waves. It has been arbitrarily divided into four stages of progressive depth.

REM sleep – so labelled because it is accompanied by occasional jerky eye movements that can be noticed under the eyelids – is associated with dreaming. It comes up every 90 minutes or so throughout the sleep period. The first REM period lasts just a few minutes, then each subsequent period increases in duration. After seven hours or so of sleep, the REM period may last 30 or more minutes, while the amount of SWS correspondingly declines in the course of the night.

Thus, the first half of the night is composed mostly of SWS, while the second half is predominantly REM. Most dreams, then, are reported from the second half of the night. The two states of sleep alternate in a rhythm produced by the release of chemicals at two different sites at the base of the brain.

There are distinct differences between the two sleep states. The most remarkable change happens in REM sleep, when the body actually becomes completely paralysed, except for the automatic process of breathing. Humans twitch slightly, just as animals do, in REM sleep. The purpose of that paralysis would seem to be to prevent us actually acting out our dreams.

In REM sleep, breathing becomes faster and is more variable than in SWS. The brain waves are fast and look "saw-toothed" on the chart record. There is penile erection in males and clitoral erection in females.

In SWS there is no muscular paralysis. Breathing is slow and steady. Conditions like sleep-walking, sleep-talking, snoring, bed-wetting and bruxism (teeth-grinding) are associated with SWS.

It used to be thought that REM sleep was essential for mental health, but certain drugs (e.g. mono-amine-oxidase/MAO inhibitor anti-depressants) completely prevent REM, yet this suppression appears to cause no deleterious effects. About half the sleep of new-born babies consists of REM, so it is possible that the state has an important function in the foetus and in early infancy, but is largely redundant in adults.

Each state of sleep has its own type of nightmare. 96 per cent of nightmares are of the REM dream variety. Heart rate and respiration increase considerably over several minutes before the sufferer awakes.

The much more rare SWS nightmare, the sleep terror, begins suddenly, with no prior indications. It is not really a dream situation, rather a sense of great fear or panic. The sufferer may have no recall at all of the event in the morning, even though the disturbance was considerable.

IDEAS ABOUT DREAMS

Dreams could be incubated in English churches up to the Middle Ages, until the witchcraft killings, when any interest in them was considered to be sorcery. Not surprisingly, they were neglected for centuries.

In the second half of the 19th century, various ideas about them began to be propounded. Robert (1866) proposed that they had a function, which was to excrete useless thoughts. Scherner (1861), long before Freud, thought that fantasy dominated the dream, free of control, and that sexual symbolism was present. Thus a clarinet could represent a penis, and a slippery footpath a vagina.

The bizarre features of dreams made them seem, superficially, to be distorted for a reason. Freud thought they were disguised wishes, which had to be modified in order to elude a Super-ego censor. The underlying, lascivious dream thoughts of the primitive Id gained expression and illusory gratification by that means.

To Freud, the purpose of the dream was to guard, or maintain sleep, but we have found that the dream actively wakens the dreamer on some occasions in order to draw attention to something in the dream.

The strong emphasis on the sexual meaning of dreams seems excessive now and may simply have been based on the known association between erections and dreaming sleep. Correlation, though, does not mean causation – studies have shown that the arousal cycle can be shifted out of phase with the REM cycle by selective awakening. The two phenomena happen at the same time, but not necessarily in a cause and effect way.

While Freud's ideas were bold and compelling, serious doubts have crept in on closer inspection.

Jung took a different tack entirely. Whereas to Freud the unconscious was a backward-looking area of repressed material, Jung saw it as forward-looking and positive. The unconscious could communicate important messages to the dreamer in the form of dreams. The function of the dream was to point out any errors in one's self-development – such as becoming too extreme in some way. Thus, a person tending to be rather pompous might dream of falling off a horse.

Adler also disagreed with Freud. He believed that both sleeping and waking thoughts are similar. He saw symbols not as disguises, but as simple representations.

Dogma has largely disappeared now in dream interpretation and has been replaced by pragmatic techniques. Our new system uses a cross-reference flow-chart method to identify the individual's personal associations with elements in the dream, and to look for consistencies, bearing in mind visual and verbal puns, in order to arrive at the dream theme.

Some theories have attempted to explain the existence of REM sleep, rather than dealing with dreaming itself. Thus, Ephron and Carrington (1966) thought that REM sleep occurs periodically to stimulate the cortex, or to clear toxins (Dement, 1964).

Evans and Newman (1958) proposed that dreams serve as a memory filter, rejecting redundant memories and responses. Dreams represent chunks of reorganized data being run through. The theory reflected an analogy with computers and appeared when it was thought that there was a need to dream. That and similar theories have now been largely discounted.

LUCID DREAMS

Lucid dreaming is an amazing experience which can be stimulated by using *The Dream Oracle* technique.

Usually in dreams we have limited critical faculties. We experience the internally generated imagery emotionally and "sensorily", but we accept without question the most bizarre happenings. However, in a lucid dream, something makes us realize that the situation could only be a dream. For instance, a person whom we know is dead might appear. At that point, a transformation occurs. Full awareness kicks in and we find ourselves conscious – yet in a phoney, but perfect, environment.

Using *The Dream Oracle*, it may occasionally happen that if you see a letter of the alphabet displayed in a dream, a similar "double-take" may occur as you suddenly remember the purpose of the incubation, and so become aware of being in an on-going dream.

A second incredible characteristic of the lucid dream is that the events can be controlled by mere thought. *What you think, you will then dream.* It is possible, say, to change the location at will, and to conjure up specific people in the dream.

Lucid dreams were hardly known until the 1970s. There had been a few obscure books describing the phenomenon, and the label "lucid" dream was introduced by Frederik van Eeden in 1913. Then, in 1968, Celia Green published *Lucid Dreams*, a book which collected cases and categorized the different characteristics.

Keith Hearne read that book, and decided to conduct the first sleep-laboratory experiments into lucid dreams. On a hunch, he thought that lucid dreamers should be able to signal information about the on-going dream to the world of wakefulness, by making coded eye-movements. Although the body is paralysed in REM sleep, the eye musculature is not inhibited.

The world's first communication from a lucid dreamer used that technique, and appeared in the polygraphic chart record on the morning of 12 April, 1975, at Hull University, England. Subsequently, Hearne moved to Liverpool University and conducted his well-known PhD research into lucid dreams, which was completed in 1978.

Dr Hearne's research proved that lucid dreams were indeed genuine dreams, occurring in REM sleep. He discovered the basic physiological findings – for instance, that lucidity is invariably preceded by an REM burst. There had been the spurious, yet commonly accepted notion that dreams were "over in a flash". Hearne's work showed that they operated in real time.

In the course of his researches, Keith Hearne also invented the first bio-feedback "dream machine", a device that provides pulses to the dreamer's wrist during dreaming (detected by respiration changes). The pulses are incorporated into the dream without causing waking, and so trigger the awareness of dreaming.

The lucid dream constitutes a wonderful "inner space" research laboratory. It is possible to conduct experiments from within the state, which has its own strange, but consistent, laws of physics.

A universal effect Dr Hearne discovered he called the "light switch effect". He found you could not increase the illumination substantially in a dream by switching on a light. But it was possible to switch a light off and then on again. This effect was tested by giving the task to lucid dreamers all over England, who reported back without biasing one another.

In the area of therapy, Hearne discovered it is possible to convert REM nightmares into pleasant lucid dreams. Most nightmare sufferers, when they detect a familiar nightmare scene appearing, tend to be on the defensive, which encourages the onset of the nightmare. Clients are taught to change their attitude to thinking, "Great! Wonderful! Here's the nightmare. That means I'm dreaming and I know I can control my dreams!" They then have a sense of mastery, and can alter the dream to their own design. Frequent nightmare sufferers have a great advantage because they can use the onset of the nightmare as a doorway into lucid dreaming.

Apart from the research and therapy aspects, the lucid dream state is very beneficial recreationally. It makes it possible to travel to exotic places, or meet famous people – all for free. It is an excellent way of relaxing and reducing stress.

The boundless creativity of the lucid dream state can also be exploited. Many works of art and scientific ideas have originated in the dream state. In the lucid dream it is possible to visit an art gallery, or enter a concert hall and hear new music.

People are now beginning to realize the enormous potential available from our dream state. Lucid dreams are the ultimate experience-engineering facility, using our inbuilt virtual reality system to explore the limitless inner universe. A chemical means may soon be developed for producing lucid dreaming. It will maintain physiological sleep, while heightening cortical arousal.

THE FALSE AWAKENING

This situation sometimes happens in dreams, especially after a lucid dream. You *dream* that you are awake. The imagery is often very vivid and you are convinced that you have just woken. But if you look around you, the surroundings are unfamiliar. Then you wake up. Very rarely there may be a few false-awakenings in sequence.

To test whether you are dreaming or not, switch on a light that you know should work. If it doesn't come on (Hearne's "light-switch effect"), it shows you are dreaming.

SLEEP PARALYSIS AND DREAM SCENERY EFFECTS

This is a curious condition where you appear to have woken and yet find yourself quite unable to move. It is, of course, a reflection of the natural bodily paralysis of REM sleep. If you relax you will sink back into REM sleep from which you will awaken normally a short time later.

Another discovery Dr Hearne made concerned the progression of visual imagery at scene-shifts. Studying hypnotic dreams, he developed a technique termed "hypno-oneirography" for externalizing the internal imagery.

On command, the dream would be stopped and "freeze-framed". Then the subject was instructed to open the eyes and, still continuing to see the still image, to project it on to a large drawing-board. The subject was next instructed to trace the scene and to describe any colours, which were later coloured in accordingly.

Using this method, the dream could be progressed little by little and a picture obtained at each halt. Eventually, a whole sequence of cartoon-like pictures revealed, vividly, the subject's personal experience of what had been seen in the dream.

Hearne found that, at scene-shifts, the pictorial elements and colours of the scene are rearranged to form a different picture. It is as if the dream progresses by a "law of least effort", along visual associative pathways.

The hypno-oneirography technique has also been used with past-life regression. A subject can be told to look at a reflective surface in the past-life scenery, and the picture is then held and traced – so resulting in a past-life portrait.

To sum up, dreaming doesn't occur the whole time throughout sleep – it happens during REM periods, which are embedded in slow wave sleep (SWS). Most REM sleep occurs in the second half of the typical night's sleep. We are paralysed when dreaming.

Freud drew attention to unconscious processes in dreams and Jung realized that the unconscious could communicate its informed opinion on current matters, via the vehicle of the dream.

There have been various adaptational approaches to explain the existence of REM sleep, but none has been greatly accepted. No one knows why we dream.

Lucid dreams are an incredible experience in which one is conscious within the dream and can control the events. It is possible that *The Dream Oracle* might trigger lucidity in some individuals.

CHAPTER 5

Divination

There are anomalous aspects of existence which indicate that, despite the apparent success of scientists to explain many things in life, there is the increasing possibility that they've got it all wrong at the most fundamental level.

Heisenberg's uncertainty principle and Gödel's theorem (the consequences of which are that physicists can never prove that a Theory of Everything is the final word on the matter) have undermined science's grandiose scheme to produce a Theory of Everything. There is, at last, the growing realization that absolutely nothing can be known with confidence – ever. Ancient Eastern teachings, which caution that all is illusion, seem now to encapsulate great, previously unrecognized, wisdom.

Science has progressed well at discovering the intricate logical processes of the created illusion, but it cannot countenance the seemingly illogical fact that the illusion might exist.

Science is highly unscientific in rejecting concepts and experiences which it cannot explain and does not wish to see because the ramifications are too self-destructive. Anomalies in the physical sciences are grasped and eagerly researched, because they suggest that the theory to date is erroneous and can be modified, but the wider reported anomalies, say, of telepathy, clairvoyance, poltergeists and precognition, are steadily ignored by a process of selective attention. That is a remarkable situation revealing a bias which will be a puzzle to future generations.

There are many self-proclaimed sceptics who talk as if science has nearly got it all sewn up and everything will be explained by an equation. Often these sceptics are authoritarian and censorious, with an almost religious fervour – in particular trying to stop the impure thought that we might not live in a physical universe. This is the ultimate blasphemy in their rigid belief system. No true scientist would, or ever could, assert that everything is explicable.

It is difficult to shake off imposed concepts. We are all indoctrinated into thinking about the world in certain ways. Dr Keith Hearne has talked and written about how he is still attempting to shake off the strait-jacket of thought in which he was placed during eight years of scientific training in psychology at three different universities, under the unacceptable and oppressive regime of Behaviourism.

ANCIENT ODDITIES

The ancients had a healthier attitude to discovering things. They observed, and made truly insightful observations unencumbered by modern theories.

There was a recurring idea that the macrocosm is reflected in the microcosm, so that what happened to a person might be mirrored in some fashion by events in nature elsewhere. Thus, the death of a king might be linked to the appearance of an unusual phenomenon.

Various divinatory techniques were developed in order to obtain information by paranormal means. There were basically two types: the interpretation of signs or omens, and communication from some knowledgeable source.

THE *I CHING*

One well-known, classical divinatory technique based on chance outcome, was the ancient Chinese *I Ching* or *Book of Changes*. Coins or yarrow sticks were tossed to produce a hexagram pattern based on male (yang) solid lines and female (yin) broken lines. Each pattern was highly symbolic and was ascribed a particular meaning. Straightforward answers were not given but the method suggested areas to be considered.

The *I Ching* was reputedly initiated in the form of trigrams by the Emperor Fo-hsi, around 2,800 BC, and developed into hexagrams by King Wen of the Chou dynasty (*circa* 1140 BC). The technique eventually reached the West in the 19th century AD. Coincidence was not considered to exist – everything was meaningful and could be interpreted. Carl Jung described such meaningful coincidences as "synchronicities".

THE DEVELOPMENT OF ASTROLOGY

This form of divination was based on the idea that the heavens influenced people. It was certainly an established system in ancient Babylonia, some 3,000 years BC. Since the movement of planets and other cosmic events could be predicted, the method was used to foretell good or bad events concerning warfare or trade.

The association between a person's birth date and what happened to that person later in life began to be formulated as the horoscope in about the 5th century BC by the Chaldeans, and later became firmly established in Greece.

Astrology was also recognized in many other ancient societies including China, Egypt and India. The practice was anathematized early in the Christian era.

In recent years, Michel Gauquelin discovered significant statistical links between people in certain professions and their birth-date. Keith Hearne has found that psychics and mediums tend to be born at the full or new moon and that persons who repeatedly sabotage their own love relationships tend to have their moon in or near Libra in the zodiac. It seems that there is much waiting to be discovered in astrology, if science will only lift its self-imposed embargo.

SCRYING

This is a universally employed form of divination where day-dream type imagery is seen, for example, on a reflective, burnished surface or speculum (catoptromancy); in a bowl of water with a drop of oil in it (hydromancy); or in a crystal ball (crystal-gazing). Good visualizers report seeing clear images which are relevant to the person seeking the consultation.

THE TAROT

This method of divination seems to be 14th-century European and uses a deck of cards in four suits: cups, swords, wands and pentacles. They may be divided into the Major Arcana archetypal (22 cards), and the Minor Arcana (56 cards). The cards are shuffled and then they are placed in a particular spread and read according to the identity of each card and its position in the spread. The overall pattern needs to be evaluated, too. The cards graphically symbolize different aspects of life and reflect a situation in the person's life at that time. They are best used with a degree of intuition.

OMENS

An omen is a happening that precedes an event or behaviour and which seems to reflect on it in some symbolic way – usually unfavourably.

The ancients carefully observed any links between things in nature and subsequent events as part of their survival. There are innumerable examples recorded in history. For instance, in the 17th century, the head of the staff of King Charles I of England fell off at his trial, and he was, of course, subsequently beheaded; and at the swearing-in of Edward, Duke of York, (father of Edward IV) a crown on a lighting contraption suddenly fell, as did a crown that stood on Dover Castle. The royal line was expected to change – and that came to pass.

Dr Hearne relates a typical modern case that he encountered, in which a 29-year-old woman, Valerie Lister, picked up her three children from school one day. While walking home with another mother and her children, a large magpie appeared and repeatedly attacked Valerie's youngest boy, four-year-old Barry. The group attempted to shoo the bird away, but it kept returning to peck at him. Later that evening,

Barry walked into the road outside his house and was killed by a vehicle.

There are many reports of loud sounds and disturbances in houses at or just before someone's death. In the 17th century, the English diarist John Aubrey collected many such accounts and included one of his own: "Three or four days before my father died, as I was in my bed about nine o'clock in the morning, perfectly awake, I did hear three distinct knocks on the bed's-head, as if it had been with a ruler or ferrula."

DREAM INCUBATION

This was a particularly important and advanced form of divination to the ancients, because it tapped into knowledge from some vast source, assumed to be the gods. Now, perhaps, apart from the individual's personal conscious and unconscious material, we would call it a cosmic Akashic record, or think it was from some collective unconscious.

The new *Dream Oracle* technique is a major development of this important divinatory process.

PREMONITIONS

A premonition is an experience which appears to anticipate a later unexpected event, and which could not reasonably have been inferred from information available beforehand. Premonitions come in various forms – waking thoughts, waking images, sleep-onset images – but the most frequent source is the dream.

These phenomena are special because they upset the scientific apple-cart regarding cause and effect. Current, orthodox science, operating under standard realism, dictates that an effect cannot precede a cause in a physical universe. Because we appear to live in a physical universe, science will not even begin to look at premonitions – they are forbidden to exist.

However, there are countless, excellent, cases of foreknowledge. The phenomenon seems to be widespread, and according to surveys, some 40 per cent of the population say they have experienced at least one premonition.

Consider the case investigated by Dr Hearne of Lesley Brennan, who had a remarkable "media announcement" type of premonition on 1 June 1974. While watching the television at noon, the word *Newsflash* appeared on the screen and a voice told of an explosion with deaths and injuries at Flixborough, a chemical plant some considerable distance away. The place meant nothing to Lesley. She told two witnesses of the explosion shortly after the newsflash. In fact, there had been no newsflash at lunchtime, because the explosion, caused by the unexpected rupturing of a 50-cm pipe, did not happen until 4.53 pm!

Barbara Garwell is another percipient studied by Hearne. Barbara has come up with many witnessed premonitions, mostly from dreams, including the assassination of President Sadat of Egypt, the attempts on the lives of President Reagan and Pope John Paul, and of many natural and man-made disasters. In many cases there has been a consistent 21-day latency period between the premonition and the later event.

Studies provide evidence strongly suggesting that premonitions actually occur. If they do happen, then by the very reasoning of science, the physical universe cannot exist, so we exist in some mind or dream world. Appearances can be deceptive. For instance, it seems obvious that the sun goes round the earth, but it is not so. Does the physical universe really exist ? It might not.

This is surely a wonderful and exhilarating new prospect to conceptualize and investigate, and one that can encompass mysteries such as telepathy, clairvoyance, miracles, synchronicities, reincarnation, and so on. But it is anathema to science.

Thus it is that the notion that nothing happens without some representation of that event occurring and being observable elsewhere has been a consistent one in human society. While it doesn't go along with what science has relatively recently dictated should be so, the ancients, lacking that stricture, and not knowing that such things were "impossible", observed cases freely and developed numerous techniques to enhance their detection.

Now that the edifice of science is crumbling and the realization is dawning that nothing is ultimately provable, we can validly look anew at ancient insights. The evidence of the existence of premonitions suggests strongly that we exist in a mind-world rather than a physical universe. Absolutely anything is possible.

Therefore, the channel of communication that has been opened by *The Dream Oracle* technique from the unconscious to the conscious mind may well convey, in addition to psychological information about the individual, data from a group mind or some cosmic record of all events. It is acceptable to an open-minded individual to request and to receive such information.

CHAPTER 6
How to Use
The Dream Oracle

*T*he *Dream Oracle* is an important, brand-new – yet simple – method for obtaining a specific comment from your unconscious on an issue that for you is unresolved. It is laid out in the form of a special dream-code related to the alphabet.

It can therefore help you decide about important matters in your life, such as a relationship, career or home, by making you aware of the wise attitude of the deep and powerful levels of consciousness within you.

That much fits within conventional psychology concerning the mind and is a clear, natural and inevitable scientific advance that will be of considerable benefit to individuals, and extremely useful to researchers and therapists.

However, the method also relates to the ancient notion that supernormal information may be accessed in dreams. It is therefore also presented as a new, very direct, form of oracle, based not on random procedures, as in auguries, but on knowledge gathered by unconscious, extra-sensory means.

In addition, because you will quickly get used to the standard dream-code, your unconscious (which is your friend, guide and adviser) will, in the future, be able to communicate important messages, either from normal or supernormal sources, to you spontaneously.

LUCID DREAMS

*T*he *Dream Oracle* can also be used as a powerful tool to initiate lucid dreams. Essentially, it involves utilizing the palpable effect of expectation and habit-forming behaviour. For example, if you wish to use the *Oracle* for this purpose, instead of concentrating your efforts on creating a message-bearing dream, ask your subconscious to provide you with a clear percentage symbol (%) in your dream imagery. Again, a certain amount of ritual must be practised. Perhaps you could take yourself off on a window-shopping trip. Every time you see a percentage sign (%) in a window, ask yourself if you are dreaming. Knowing that you are wide awake is irrelevant. The important criterion here is that you will be developing the habit of assessing your state of consciousness. Eventually, you will indeed be presented with the percentage sign in a dream. If then, as part of habitual behaviour, you ask yourself if you are dreaming, you will realize that you are. The moment this is established, you will be fully conscious within your dream – in other words, lucid. Then the miracle of lucid dreams will be made available to you and you will find you can take control over your dreams. You can then experience a wealth of fantasy adventures — such as flying, or becoming involved in a romantic encounter, or you may use the time to evoke healing.

The significance of *The Dream Oracle* is enormous to you. It will help you for life.

OUR METHOD

This new technique provides the unconscious with a simple but direct language. Its messages are actually distorted by the usual dream-producing process — hence the necessity for interpretation — but here the unconscious can use a simple pointer to reveal its opinion, by emphasizing a particular letter of the alphabet in a dream.

Essentially, before sleep, you need to select and concentrate on the matter requiring resolution, on which you want your unconscious to give its opinion, and carefully familiarize yourself with the dream alphabet code and the full meanings.

On waking, you should write down full accounts of your dreams and identify the letter being communicated. You may actually see a letter in the dream, or you may notice that many objects or names of people in the dream begin with the same letter.

Once the code letter is established, consult the full *Dream*

Oracle meanings and consider how the message relates to your question. The relevant part of the stated meaning will be recognized readily.

Very occasionally, there may be more than one letter communicated in the same dream, and sometimes the message may come a day or two *after* the incubation – so don't be too impatient for a response.

The first time you try out *The Dream Oracle* you may not have a specific question and yet you may find that your subconscious is providing a communication to you anyway.

When you select the unresolved problem, make it very simple and on one topic only. It is useful to write the issue on a piece of paper and place it under your pillow. That focuses your mind clearly on the matter.

It is also a good idea to write the dream alphabet words in a list and place it near your bed, so that it acts as a prompter to your subconscious. The act of typing or writing the words will also assist their recognition and integration into your subconscious mind.

If you wake up suddenly in the night from a dream, it is likely that your subconscious will have caused that awakening so that you can recall a significant dream. This deliberate waking by the subconscious has been termed the "trigger effect" by David Melbourne.

It is best to record your dream immediately with a small hand-held recorder. Don't switch on the light initially, simply give a commentary on the dream, then sit up and write a full account, referring to the voice recording. We would strongly advise you to keep a dream diary, as an on-going record of your dreams. You will find that your recall of dreams steadily increases if you write them down.

Always be on the look-out for spontaneously provided messages when you have not deliberately consulted *The Dream Oracle*. Your subconscious may consider, occasionally, that although it has not been requested to give advice, a certain matter deserves its comment.

THE DREAM ALPHABET CODE LIST

Overleaf is the list of 26 words, each related to a letter of the alphabet, that forms the basis of *The Dream Oracle* technique. Look carefully at each one. If possible memorize the list, in order to establish the range of possible dream answers in your mind.

You also need to read carefully the full message associated with each alphabetical letter, presented in Part Two of this book.

The letters constitute a set of specific answers from which your subconscious mind can select one that is particularly relevant to the question you ask before sleep.

AVARICE	NATURE
BREVITY	OVER-USE
CONSEQUENCE	PATIENCE
DIVINITY	QUEST
ENVY	REPENTANCE
FAITH	SLOTH
GREED	TALENT
HOPE	UNDERSTANDING
IRE	VANITY
JOY	WILL
KARMA	X-RAY
LUST	YESTERDAY
MEDITATION	ZEN

WHEN TO USE *THE DREAM ORACLE*

You should use the *Oracle* when you find yourself in a situation where you need the wise counsel of your subconscious, which has access to much more relevant data than you possess consciously. This might be when you are unsure about an important decision that you have to make, about a job or career, a relationship, a house move, a holiday, or any other matter where you are not sure quite what to do.

WHEN NOT TO USE *THE DREAM ORACLE*

Do not abuse this special technique. Some people greatly over-use the *I Ching*, the tarot, the runes, and other divinatory methods to the point where they employ them daily to make the simplest decisions. It is wrong to become over-dependent on such systems. Do not attempt to use it unethically for financial gain or control over others.

To counter over-dependence on *The Dream Oracle*, we have designated the letter "O" to represent Overuse. Take care if the letter is portrayed to you in a dream.

LEVELS OF INCUBATION

The degree of importance of your request for a response to a question may be conveyed to your subconscious mind by the amount of preparation and ritual that is employed beforehand. As we have seen in the chapter on dream incubation, ritual enhances psychological expectation.

Six increasing levels of incubation are shown on the following pages. It is probably best to start with a lower level incubation; the more complex ones may not be necessary. For a major life change, look at the higher levels for your dream response.

LEVEL ONE INCUBATION

This is the minimum way of using *The Dream Oracle*. Read the book, to obtain background knowledge, and in particular, carefully inspect the Dream Alphabet Code List on page 78 and the full Dream Alphabet information in Part Two.

Those steps will effectively be like entering a programme, and data, into a computer. Your subconscious mind will assimilate and store the information. You may have quite a feeling of elation, too – the subconscious will realize that it has, at last, a simple and straightforward way of letting you know important things consciously.

LEVEL TWO INCUBATION

This involves slightly more work on the part of the incubant. Do everything stated in Level One: carefully inspect the Dream Alphabet Code List on page 78 and the full Dream Alphabet information in Part Two. Now bring in a little ritual, such as writing or printing the Alphabet Code List and placing it by your bed.

Also write down or print the unresolved problem, which must be very specific and unambiguous, and place it under your pillow.

In addition, make more effort to record your dreams. Note them down on waking.

LEVEL THREE INCUBATION

Here, carry out all the procedures of Levels One and Two Incubation. Now add two further elements.

Firstly, actually learn the Alphabetic Code List so that you can recite it without hesitation. Secondly, say aloud the following Prayer of Protection to add a sense of significance to the proceedings:

The Prayer of Protection

Let a point of light within my inner core
Expand and shine through every cell of me
And purify my soul.
Let a shell of light surround my earthly form
And create a dazzling outer shield of goodness
So evil won't come near.
Let the universal light stream from its source
And show to me the landscape all around,
And let the light reveal to me the truth.
Let the overwhelming love that knows no bounds
Flow into and from my heart for ever,
And may the powers of darkness hasten away.
Let love, and light, and good
Protect me evermore.

LEVEL FOUR INCUBATION

This is a more determined approach, incorporating all the previous material, with the addition of some ritual and an invocation. Carry out all the procedures described above for Levels One to Three, including the Prayer of Protection. If you are practised in self-hypnosis, utilize that state to enhance the self-suggestion of a significant dream.

Suggested ritual procedure:

- In the evening, do not eat (if medically acceptable).
- Drink only pure water.
- Burn incense and wear simple, loose, clean clothes.
- Sit quietly and think about the matter that requires resolution.
- Before sleep, bathe and apply scented oils to the body.
- Sleep in a freshly made bed.

Invocation:

Repeat this wording to yourself until you fall asleep.

I ask my unconscious mind
Which recalls all that has ever happened to me,
And which knows my deepest thoughts and motives,
And which has access to even wider information,
To provide me with a clear answer in a vivid dream tonight
to the matter which I wish to be resolved.

LEVEL FIVE INCUBATION

This method should be used if you wish to make a very serious attempt to obtain important guidance from your unconscious. Follow all the procedures described for Levels One to Four, and in addition, have a special rest day before the incubation night. On that day, follow these instructions:

- Start the day by bathing and cleansing your whole body.
- Burn incense and wear simple, loose, clean clothes.
- Do not eat (if medically acceptable).
- Drink only pure water.
- Several times during the day, sit quietly and think about the matter that needs to be resolved.
- Bathe again before sleep and apply scented oils to the body.
- Sleep in a freshly made bed.

LEVEL SIX INCUBATION

This ultimate form of incubation requires that you sleep at a special sacred place in order to receive your inner message. Of course, you must get permission to do so, and consider your personal safety.

Include the procedures already described and any other kind of ceremonial ritual that you instinctively feel might be useful, such as drumming, chanting, and so on.

Part Two

THE STANDARD, UNIVERSAL,
ALPHABETIC DREAM CODE

A
AVARICE

Perhaps apples, antelopes, apes, angels or arms were prominent in your dream? Or maybe you dreamt of an avalanche, or of receiving an accolade or advice? You might have been an actor, or in an audience watching actors. You might have heard the name Adam being shouted out. Whatever, if you feel the prominent feature in your dream represented the letter "A", then you have turned to the correct page.

The first thing that springs to mind when we see the word avarice is greed for wealth or possessions. But there are many other associations which apply to avarice, so do not be disheartened because your dream has brought you to this page. Remember, your subconscious has understood the purpose of this divinatory system, and is alerting you to the need to identify with one of those same associations.

If you are not lusting after money and cannot connect yourself with the conventional meaning of avarice, then keep reading, because, as you progress through the following paragraphs, the message behind the dream will be revealed. You will sense when you have come to the right place in the text, there will be a feeling of familiarity.

However, if you are able to identify with the recognized meaning of avarice, then your subconscious is telling you that your pursuit of wealth is taking over your life, to the detriment of your own development and perhaps of those around you.

There is nothing wrong in striving for a better standard of living providing that others do not get hurt along the way. Your subconscious wants you to stand back and look objectively at your life, to be honest with yourself. Is your pursuit of material wealth becoming an obsession? Are people around you being affected?

If the answer is yes, then your subconscious is alerting you to the fact that you are thinking too much with the left side of your brain, the side associated with cold calculation. You need to strike a better balance by taking part in some sort of pastime which will stimulate the right side of the brain, which is allied to intuition and creativity – perhaps a hobby such as painting, writing, meditation, or simply listening to music. Or maybe you like walking, sailing, gardening or sport?

You must take some time out for yourself and consider what effect your recent activities have been having on those around you. Slow down a little, and you will be surprised at how much more fulfilling life can be.

If, however, you are unable to relate to the above, ask yourself whether your subconscious is reinforcing your belief that the emphasis society places on money is responsible for much which is wrong with the world. In your case, is the dream giving you a nudge to take some positive action?

Perhaps you have been contemplating becoming involved in charity work, but have always found an excuse to put it off? Is there an aged neighbour nearby, or a relative in need of help? Just a simple act to demonstrate that money is not the be all and end all can make the world of difference to somebody's life.

You might be aware of a child, or somebody in your family or work environment, who is being driven by avarice. In this case your dream is telling you to be aware. Consider whether it might be advantageous to lead by example. Demonstrate to them in some way that, in the long run, a benevolent heart reaps more rewards than wealth could ever match.

Or could it be that you are making unwarranted demands on a partner or friend for material gain? Stop and think about it. The other side of the coin prompts you to ask yourself if you have been pandering to somebody else's greed, perhaps for love or the desire to be liked. True love and friendship do not come through material wealth.

Perhaps your subconscious has identified something in your life which is beginning to become a temptation to you? Give the matter some thought and ask yourself if it is worth the sacrifice that might be necessary to achieve that particular goal.

Whatever the reason for your dream, look around you and you will find the reason why your subconscious has alerted you to avarice.

B
BREVITY

If your dream centred on the letter "B" – maybe you dreamt of bats, balls, beetles, bison or buffalo – your attention is drawn to Brevity, which indicates being to the point, concise, or cut short.

Perhaps there is a situation in your life that has been dragging on for too long, when nothing productive is happening, and where only negative energies are at work. Maybe you have been suffering in silence, almost imperceptibly drawn into a rut. If this description sounds familiar, then your subconscious is telling you that the time has come to be decisive, to dispense with diplomacy for diplomacy's sake, and be honest with yourself. There is a way out of the situation which can be achieved without hurting somebody else. Meditate on the problem and the answer will be revealed.

However, there are many facets to brevity. Have you recently been impolite and curt to a loved one, friend or acquaintance? Have you been preoccupied with yourself, to the detriment of others? If so, consider how you can make amends.

The dream might be a warning to those who have a contract to sign and are tempted to go ahead without proper consideration. Resist the temptation to sign on the dotted line. Ignore those around you who are urging you to comply, and seek advice from a source who will be able to see the facts beneath the veneer of temptation. It might be that just one clause needs altering, but it will be one of significance. So if you are faced with a contract and the "B" featured prominently in your dream, you are being urged to use caution.

On the other hand, have you an inner knowledge that you have been erring on the side of caution in a situation which, unless acted upon with decisiveness, might pass you by? Perhaps somebody has extended the hand of friendship and is offering you something for nothing. It could be a business proposition, or an invitation to a party. Whatever, your subconscious is telling you to verify your inner feelings of trust, then act positively before the boat of destiny sails for the open sea.

Perhaps there is an emotional crisis where you feel you are being pressured to make a snap decision? Ask yourself if some sort of emotional blackmail is being used in an attempt to make you act hastily. Then the dream is telling you to stand firm. Quietly withdraw from a confrontation by stalling for time in which to do some clear-headed thinking away from the emotional ties. View the situation as dispassionately as you can. Take your time and a solution will present itself.

Or do you suspect that you have been short-changed in return for some sort of contribution which was worth far more? It might be a situation at home, at work, or in a place of leisure. Then this is a cautionary dream which is urging you to recognize any similar situation which might present itself in the future. Learn by your mistakes and acknowledge the dream's message.

Conversely, have you short-changed somebody else, been less

than fair with them? If so, although you might have fooled your conscious into thinking that it does not matter, your subconscious and even your conscience know better. The message here is to make amends and put things right. You will know how to go about it.

Are you engaged in a project you are tiring of, and are tempted to cut short by rushing to finish? Perhaps it is no more than completing a menial task like a repair job. Or it could be something far more substantial like putting together a business package. If you can identify with this description and are reading this section as a result of your dream, then pay attention. A slapdash job could lead to accidents, or the loss of a business account. You are being urged to look at things from a different perspective. See the sense in the benefits of job satisfaction and see it through with care and determination. The proof of the pudding will be in the results, whether you listen to the message in your dream or not!

Remember, in one form or another, brevity is the message. If you are unable to empathize with any of the above examples, do some serious thinking, because your own subconscious surely knows better!

C
CONSEQUENCES

Did you dream of the letter "C" on its own, or was your dream packed with objects and characters each beginning with this letter: cannons, cattle, canoes, clams or, perhaps, crickets?

Clearly, a dream which has featured strongly enough to have prompted you to turn to this page might be very important. It is also likely to demand some deep thinking on your part to identify the message to which your subconscious is trying to alert you. Every single thing that happens in life might result, by necessity, in unlimited consequences. For every action there is a reaction.

Consider the domino effect, and so it is with everything in life, whether seen or unseen, heard or unheard, known or unknown, recognized or unrecognized. Everything you do in life has an effect on something or somebody else, or a combination of both. Like the circular ripples in a pond, every decision you make will, inevitably, have consequences!

Ponder on the following story. A man decides to write a letter to his friend arranging a meeting, then forgets to post it. Immediately, there are consequences, even as a result of the act of forgetting.

If his friend had received the letter, he might have made alternative arrangements for the day of the intended meeting. However, because the letter never arrived, like a steam train with a full head of steam, an unstoppable sequence of consequences are likely to have been set in motion. Everything his friend now does during that day would have had a different outcome and different consequences had they met.

Consider a worst-case scenario, perhaps his friend takes his usual train which crashes, or drives to work as usual and runs somebody over. Of course, it would not be the fault of the person who forgot to post the letter, but, nevertheless, this does illustrate exactly how many combinations of cause and effect could occur as a direct result of an unconscious decision or omission. Therefore, even non-action has a consequence.

Remember, everybody whom the friend is likely to encounter that day will experience some sort of consequence, even if it is merely shaking hands. In turn, that might be the cause of that person being a second or two late for his bus, which might cause him to run across the road to catch a taxi. Depending on whether he makes it across the road safely it will either have consequences for an unsuspecting taxi driver, or a team of doctors and nurses at the local casualty department.

And all these people also have families and people with whom they are going to interact, also resulting in a chain of consequence. So there are literally limitless combinations of consequences for each action or inaction we experience. For these kinds of consequences, there can be no blame attributed. Forgetting to post a letter is hardly a punishable offence, is it?

But there is a far more serious side to the subject of consequence. Each thought you have could be a blueprint for reality. You only have to act on that thought and you have set what might be an unstoppable series of consequences in motion. A series that, had you stopped to think about it, could have avoided some very negative outcomes, that maybe you could have foreseen.

Now consider the reason your subconscious has sent you a dream which has resulted in you turning to the subject of consequences. Are you on the brink of making a decision which could lead to some harmful consequences to yourself or somebody else?

Perhaps you are aware of a loved one, friend, or colleague who is talking about taking some sort of action. Is your dream telling you to think of all of the possible consequences of such an action?

Or could it be something as innocent as posting a letter or making a phone call? Remember, things you don't do also lead to consequences, so this time, is your dream merely serving as a reminder?

Your subconscious is telling you to think deeply about things surrounding your life now, and consider the consequences. You never know, such meditation might save a life, or simply cheer somebody up. Nevertheless, do think specifically about actions you have considered taking, and their consequences.

D
DIVINITY

Perhaps your dream presented itself with the obvious symbolism of the divine, or maybe it was something more mundane, such as the representation of a doll, daffodil, dandelion, duck, dragon or even a dormouse. However, to have the letter "D" prominent in your dream is an invitation for you to pay attention to spiritual matters.

You do not have to belong to a church or view yourself as being particularly religious to have been prompted by your dream to turn to this page. In fact, you might even consider yourself to be an atheist. Nevertheless, your subconscious has of its own accord recognized the need for you to consider certain aspects of spirituality.

Some claim that when we die, that is the end of everything, there is no such thing as the soul. If you share these views do not be surprised that you are reading this section. This book is not designed to interfere with your beliefs. But ask yourself if you can deny the existence of the conscience?

Interestingly, though, near-death experiences and war, specifically, have taught us that when death threatens, even the most seemingly strident atheists often call for God's help!

However, it is the conscience which draws the line between good and evil. Every healthy-minded person will be able to relate to an event in their life when their conscience told them that they had done wrong. So, exactly what is the conscience?

The atheist might believe that the conscience represents a logical path of thought patterns which discriminates between right and wrong. The spiritually minded might regard the conscience as the inner voice, perhaps of God. Whatever the theory, none of us can deny the existence of the conscience and the purpose it serves.

If you are not religious or view yourself as an atheist then your dream is alerting you to a matter of conscience. Give some thought to an event or a situation which is prominent in your life right now, or is likely to feature very soon. Then examine your motivation in the role you are planning to execute in these circumstances. Be honest with yourself and ask if you are acting or intending to act against your conscience.

On the other hand, your dream might be alerting you to a loved-one, friend or colleague, whom you know to be behaving in a manner which is less than honourable. If this is the case, you are being asked by your subconscious to consider whether it is right for you to turn a blind eye, or perhaps help that person to see the error of his or her ways.

However, if recently you have been questioning your non-spiritual stance in life, then this dream represents a turning point for you. You will recognize instinctively the calling for you to search for God. You will understand your unconscious desire to tread the path of love and understanding. Under these circumstances, your dream will have changed your life forever! The time is now right for you to open your heart to God and allow Him to enter.

For those who consider themselves to be spiritually aware,

or on the road to enlightenment, your subconscious has brought you this dream regardless of what religion you follow.

Perhaps you are following your religion to the point of fanaticism? Ask yourself if your quest for enlightenment has taken over your life to the extent where others around you are being hurt as a result. If you have been pursuing religious beliefs to the detriment of all else, then your dream is urging you to temper your commitment with a little love and understanding of those around you.

Conversely, have you been neglecting your spiritual development recently? Perhaps, unwittingly, you have been sucked into the pervading desire to surround yourself with material attributes. Is your yearning for physical benefits selling you short? If these words strike a chord, then it is time for you to get back on the rails, and pursue more important things in life.

Has somebody you know been showing an interest in spiritual matters? If the answer is yes, then this dream is telling you to point them in the right direction, or introduce them to somebody else who can.

Perhaps your dream wants you to take a closer look within yourself, to review your life and ask if you are going in the right direction. Stop and think, ask yourself if you are treading the right path. Are your loved ones, friends and colleagues content with you, or might certain aspects of your inner self be causing these people to suffer in silence?

If you are happy with your review of yourself, perhaps this dream is giving you a pat on the back and encouraging you to continue just the way you are.

Maybe you are going through a period when your faith is being tested? You may have found yourself in a situation of great mental anguish. Illness in the family or in a close friend often has the effect of weakening one's faith. Or perhaps there are difficult financial troubles, or maybe nothing seems to have gone right recently.

Often, under these circumstances, people wonder that if there is a God, how could He allow such awful things to happen? All religions share a belief in a better place, but none seems to answer the question. However, are there some words to be found in the Bible, for instance, which might give us a clue?

It is not our intention to interpret the Lord's Prayer, but could one particular phrase be suggesting an answer? "Thy Kingdom come, Thy will be done." Could these words be implying that, until His Kingdom does come, His will cannot be done on earth as it is in heaven? Until that day comes, is the planet and all who dwell thereon left to their own devices, to wreak as much or little havoc as free will allows?

If these words make sense to you, then your dream is asking you to give these matters some thought, and draw comfort from the conclusions you reach. Under these circumstances, your subconscious is offering you a way to bolster your faith and grow in love and understanding.

Whatever reason your dream focused on the "D", your subconscious knew it would lead you to this section in the book. If none of the paragraphs seems appropriate, then your dream is asking that you look deeper for the answer. If you make the effort, it will be revealed.

E
ENVY

The letter "E" might have come to you in your dream in many forms. Maybe you dreamt of elephants, eels, engines, elbows, elves or elastic. There is no need to despair because your dream has brought you the letter "E". There are many facets to envy, and some you may not have considered previously.

However, it might be a straightforward case of envy. If you have found yourself suffering from this undesirable feeling recently, then your subconscious is indicating that you are seeing things from the wrong perspective. It is telling you to be thankful for what you have got.

Perhaps the object of your envy is something with roots in the material world? There are many more things than material gain to be thankful for: a loving husband or wife, children, family, friendship and good health are things which readily spring to mind. If you enjoy one or perhaps all of these, then you have much that others could be envying.

Material gains end at the grave, but love and friendship are able to transcend death, even if they survive merely in the form of a memory. But for those who believe, love is the only eternal thing that exists – all else passes away. If these words seem to strike a familiar chord, then your dream is telling you to be happy in love, friendship and good health – there are many who are far worse off than you. Cheer up and get on with your life!

However, if you live alone and the objects of your envy are those named above, do not despair – you are not alone. Consider what you see when you look out of the window: the sky, living nature in one form or another. There is joy to be found in the miracle of life itself. Your dream is urging you to take stock, and look for the positive aspects in your life.

Perhaps you find pleasure in music, reading, writing, watching the television, walking, going to the shops and meeting people, or in a creative pastime? Your dream is reassuring you not to feel despair, because there is more to life than you might realize. Look deeper for the answer and you will find it.

If you are in the fortunate position to live life in relative comfort, there is nothing wrong with that. But your dream is reminding you how fortunate you are, and how damaging it could be to those who are less happy, if you flaunt your good fortune. This dream is reminding you of the attributes associated with living unpretentiously.

Envy too often starts early and contaminates the innocence of childhood, tainting a balanced development. Look around you, is envy taunting a child you know? If the answer is yes, then this dream is alerting you to the fact that you are in a position to rectify the situation.

If it is your own children who are involved in sibling rivalry born out of envy, then your subconscious is reminding you that sometimes, even unconsciously, we can make fish of one and fowl of another. Often it is not always material gifts which invoke envy. Ask yourself if recently you have praised one child and ignored another.

Remember how sensitive children are, and how easily they can feel left out. Under these circumstances, a word in the right place can banish feelings of envy and bring harmony to a damaged ego.

If none of these examples seems appropriate to your circumstances, bear in mind that your dream brought you the "E" for a reason. Envy can manifest itself in many other forms, so give due consideration to the reasons that inevitably lie behind the dream and you will find the answer.

F
FAITH

If the letter "F" featured strongly in your dream, perhaps through continued appearances of a father figure, faces, flags, fences or even a fish, then you have turned to the correct page.

In this book, "D = Divinity" deals with faith of a religious nature, but this section considers other aspects. In this sense, faith can often be allied to trust, and can apply to numerous life situations.

If you suffer from low self-esteem and are constantly undervaluing yourself, at last, through *The Dream Oracle*, your subconscious has found a way of shouting a message to you: HAVE FAITH IN YOURSELF, TRUST IN YOUR ABILITIES TO SUCCEED, BELIEVE IN YOURSELF!

The time has arrived for you to kick the habit of putting yourself down. No longer take the back seat in decision making. Don't be frightened of what others might say as a result of you expressing your own opinions and ideas. Go for it! You will be surprised how readily people will appear willing to listen to your views.

However, to sound persuasive, first you have to believe in yourself. Each night, when you retire and enter the nodding-off stage of sleep, keep telling yourself that you have faith in your own abilities. Continually reinforce this suggestion throughout each and every day, and you will soon come to realize your considerable potential.

If you have ample self-confidence, this dream might be telling you to have faith in somebody else. Maybe somebody close to you is embarking on a venture which concerns you. It could be that one of your children is preparing to leave home for university, or even something more minor like taking a first solo trip to the shops. Your subconscious is telling you that the time has come to have faith in their ability – do not worry.

Perhaps you are in two minds over an issue which hinges on advice you have received. If this sounds familiar, then your subconscious is urging you to trust your intuition, make a decision accordingly and have faith that things will work out.

Sometimes, things do not go according to plan and seem to backslide somewhat. Nevertheless, persist with the trust in your original decision and witness how things often have a way of working out, albeit in an unexpected way.

Or is somebody in your life putting too much faith in you? Perhaps they are not standing on their own two feet. If this description rings a bell, then your dream is alerting you to the fact that it is time that you took a step back and encouraged that person to be more independent.

Conversely, you might feel frustrated because somebody is not showing enough faith in your abilities. For example, a supervisor at work might be looking over your shoulder continually. This aspect of faith (or lack of it), could apply to countless other instances. Then it is time to make a stand by explaining tactfully that you are able to function efficiently. Even better, select the appropriate moment and circumstance and prove it.

Or perhaps right now your faith in human nature is being tested? If so, then measure all the good that is done in the world against less positive aspects of humanity. Take heart in the fact that there are countless people who give of their time and money to help others. Some may risk their lives by driving convoys of food through war-ravaged countries, while others might be offering prayers for world peace.

Be reassured that although the world seems to be in a state of upheaval, the damage is nearly always done by the minority. Most people want to live in peace and harmony and are often quite willing to lend a helping hand.

The fact that you have been drawn to this section of the book is a sign that you should ponder the many facets to the subject of faith, then the true meaning of your dream will spring to mind.

G
GREED

If you were led to this page by dreaming predominantly of gates, gnats, girls, guillotines, glass, giants or gnomes, then the letter "G" is signifying an aspect of greed, which need not carry a detrimental meaning. Indeed, greed is often associated with hunger, therefore there are many connotations which can be attached to the subject.

Recently, perhaps, you may have overcome a particular challenge and now, after the event, feel somewhat deflated. Under these circumstances are you able to identify with a craving for a new obstacle that will put your skills to the test? If so, then this dream is calling on you to be patient. A new challenge will present itself in due course. In the meantime, however, reflect on the last experience and take the opportunity to benefit from the lessons you learned.

Are you involved in some sort of learning process or study course? Maybe you feel that you have grasped the basics of the subject matter already and are eager to get on with the more detailed aspects – hungry for knowledge? If this rings a bell, your subconscious is urging caution. Go over what you have previously covered, because you might have overlooked an important basic principle which could lead to a long-term flaw in your understanding of the whole picture.

A more obvious meaning for greed could simply relate to food consumption. Ask yourself if you are guilty of overindulgence? If this strikes a chord, your dream carries an important message. Examine the reasons that lie behind your eating habits. Are you comfort eating? In any event, your dream is alerting you to the obvious pitfalls and risks attached to over-eating which, if allowed to continue unchecked, might be waiting for you a few years along the road.

Your subconscious is clearly concerned and is drawing your attention to a problem. If you feel that you are unable to curtail your desire for food, then seek help. Be aware that your subconscious has recognized a problem and knows that you are capable of finding a solution.

Do you know of somebody in your life who shares some sort of benefit with you, at home, socially or in the workplace? Perhaps you are aware that this person persistently takes more than their fair share of these advantages. Discretion is called for, but be firm.

Maybe greed is driving somebody to take advantage of your good nature? Remember, sometimes it does not help to allow things to continue – too much sugar decays the teeth!

Is your dream pointing to certain aspects of your own personality, where, driven by greed, you are exploiting something or somebody else? Stop and think of the long-term consequences. Reward now may result in loss further down the road.

Do you know somebody who is suffering at the hands of greed? If you do, then your dream is alerting you to the possibility that you might hold the answer to that person's problem. Give the matter some thought and if this definition applies to you, an amicable solution can be found.

Greed can manifest itself in so many different ways, so if the above examples do not seem to apply to your present circumstances, bear in mind that your subconscious is trying to bring you a message that specifically pertains to greed. If you look hard enough, you will know instinctively when you have found the aspect of greed which brought you your dream.

H
HOPE

Did you play hopscotch in your dream? Remember, dreams can play on words, and hope is one of those words which lends itself to more than one type of dream deception. The word "hop" is very close to "hope", but in addition, the act of hopping can easily be allied to that of hoping. Perhaps there were more direct symbols, such as horses, houses, hearts, hills, hinges or a predominance of handles in your dream.

Whatever device your subconscious ingeniously used, your dream has brought you to the letter "H" to clarify how hope relates to you.

Have you been down on your luck recently, when nothing seemed to go right? Perhaps you found yourself out of work, or that unexpected bill landed on your mat. If you think that no matter what you do, some sort of invisible force is bearing down on you just to keep you at the bottom of the pile, your dream is telling you in no uncertain terms that you are wrong! In fact, your subconscious has the answer to your problems.

We are all familiar with the saying that it never rains but it pours. This suggests that bad luck usually comes in large doses – when you're down you're likely to be kicked. Does this description sound familiar?

The truth is that you have probably been reacting in a manner which serves to invite a sort of self-fulfilling prophecy of doom and gloom. When we are hit by a negative force, several things can happen. Our demeanour is likely to change physically. Some may walk around wearing an expression resembling thunder, which conveys the message, "Keep away!". Others might tend to become withdrawn, the message being, "My misery rubs off!". So it is not by accident that when it rains it pours.

Unlike a magnet, where opposites attract, the reverse is true of emotions. Negative forces always invite negative outcomes. Just as laughter can be contagious, the same applies to misery. Therefore it is not surprising that others are likely to keep their distance – they are automatically repelled.

There are many sayings which allude to the opposite side of the coin: "Money goes to money," or "Success breeds success," for example. It is no mistake that we sometimes hear stories about people who have been unemployed for an extended period, only to discover that, suddenly, they are offered two or three jobs within days of each other.

Just as laughter can be contagious, so can a positive attitude. People are far more likely to be forthcoming with assistance if they are dealing with somebody who responds positively, instead of with an air of impending disaster. Therefore, whether you are faced with unemployment, debt, experiencing problems in affairs of the heart, or just seem down on your luck, stop and think.

There may be more to this attitude than the way you present yourself to other people. Consider other circumstances which appear to have no connection with being given a leg-up. We all recognize the person who seems to be on a winning streak in games of chance. Often, these same people report that they experienced something more than just positive thinking – they seemed to know they were going to win, which led to a feeling approaching elation.

They all seem to have something in common – they are usually in a happy mood at the time. Although there is no scientific evidence to support the claim that if one is happy, then by some sort of magic, luck will begin to improve, there is plenty of anecdotal evidence which seems to suggest that this is indeed the case.

Consider that, before you had your dream, you read through this book. Now ponder why your dream brought you to the letter "H". Your subconscious has identified a situation in your life that could be improved by thinking positively, giving out the appropriate vibes, and invoking happiness by looking on the bright side.

Try to work out how you can turn a disadvantage into an advantage. Try looking for a silver lining to that black cloud, then act on it in a positive way. Change your mind-set from doom and gloom to one of hope! Remember, your subconscious has absorbed this book and brought you this message, so this approach stands a good chance of working. No matter how dire your situation, hang on to hope and you stand a good chance of turning things around.

I
IRE

Were you aware of eyes, ice, Ireland, Indians, ink, irises, incense or something else featuring the letter "I" in your dream, which prompted you to turn to this page?

Ire, or anger, is something common to everybody, so don't be surprised that your dream has alerted you to it. If this is the first time you have used *The Dream Oracle* you are likely to have forgotten the meaning attributed to the "I". However, don't doubt your dream, because when you picked up the book, you were certain enough to turn to this page – so read on.

Perhaps your subconscious is telling you that you should be angry about something. Have you recently witnessed some sort of injustice and kept quiet about it? If you can relate to this, then your dream is telling you to be angry. Not to the point of losing your temper, however, but just enough to spur you into action.

Under certain circumstances, it may be prudent to keep a still tongue, but your dream is informing you that, in this instance, you can do something about it that will result in a satisfactory conclusion. There is a way in which you can redress the balance and see justice served.

Your subconscious is telling you to allow your anger to have its place, but to keep a cool head. This way, anger can be harnessed and put to positive use. There is a way in which you can achieve your goal without hurting anybody, yet at the same time, rectify a wrong. Give this matter some deep thought and the answer will be revealed. But remember you must become master over your anger and channel it in a positive, constructive way, calmly and diligently. Never allow anger to become master over you!

Perhaps you have taken some sort of inappropriate action which is going to provoke an angry response in somebody else? If so, your dream is telling you not to over-react when that response comes – you brought it upon yourself. Acknowledge that you made a mistake and apologize.

If you are still in a position where you can undo the error of your judgement before it is discovered, and if you have been having doubts about your deed, you are being told to rectify the situation before it is too late – you may have underestimated the seriousness of the consequences.

Maybe you are suffering from an injustice yourself, and anger has been getting the better of you? If this sounds familiar, your dream is pointing out that, eventually, things will settle down. You are being urged to look at the situation from a different perspective.

Is the perpetrator of the injustice aware of all the facts, or did he or she act in good faith? If there is any doubt in your mind, calm down and think of ways in which you can bring all the facts to light.

On the other hand, if you are unable to equate with the above scenario, your dream is underpinning your own knowledge that simmering anger is a negative force which, if allowed to continue unchecked, can have a direct bearing on your physical and mental health. You need to let off some steam in a constructive manner.

Perhaps you are physically able and can vent your frustration on a playing field or in the local gymnasium. Perhaps a brisk walk or even a spot of gardening might take your mind off things. Whatever your circumstances, you are being reminded that unless you regain control and your equilibrium, you are courting danger in one form or another.

Unless anger is made to serve in a positive way, it is a destructive force with very few attributes. History provides us with much evidence which shows that peace made out of anger is rarely long-lasting. Change your mind-set and with it be in control of your own destiny.

Occasionally, ire can be a constructive servant, but it is always a destructive master!

J
JOY

Perhaps you were jogging in your dream, or studying jockeys astride their mounts, or admiring jewels, witnessing jesters, jade, jam or jackals. Whatever it was, the important thing is that your dream featured the letter "J".

Joy could be one of the most significant messages your subconscious is communicating to you. A powerful emotion, joy is linked to love and represents an opposing aspect to anger born out of hate. Joy is a very positive force which often brings healing with it.

If you are not particularly religious, there is significant scientific evidence which suggests that laughter born out of joy stimulates the body's immune system. Feeling fit and healthy can promote more feelings of happiness, creating a sort of self-perpetuating system. Do not underestimate the positive power of joy.

If, however, you are religious, then remember that happiness and laughter born out of joy are music to God's ears. Joy, when linked to love, has tremendous potential to heal mind, body, spirit and, ultimately, the planet too. The more thoughts of love we are able to send out, the more joy is brought into the world. Like the ripples in a pool of water, joy has the potential to spread its healing power. Whatever your religious persuasion, it cannot be denied that the world would be a much nicer place for all concerned if more people displayed this beautiful emotion.

Consider why humans are prepared to spend vast amounts of money to be made happy – throughout the world comedy is a multi-million dollar industry. But why, through the media of television, cinema, or radio, do we go to such expense to experience feelings of happiness, when, with very little effort, we can have it for nothing?

Just as bad moods rub off on to somebody else, so does happiness, which is why laughter can be considered contagious. We all know that witnessing an event which is surrounded with joy can be uplifting, and these experiences usually lead to feelings of well-being.

The link between joy and love is no mistake. Consider the possible results, if people were to smile a lot of the time, offer a helping hand to one another and give out love. We often hear about how close those people were who lived through the blitz during the Second World War. Even during those horrific times, people found feelings of joy born out of love. Many stories abound about people's humour when faced with despair and adversity. Is it coincidence, then, that many stories exist about how these same people shared feelings of love for one another?

For reasons known only to you, your subconscious has brought you a dream so you can ponder the attributes of joy. Perhaps there is somebody close to you who needs the healing power of laughter? Consider, then, how best to bring them that gift. If your heart is not in it, the transparent veneer of false happiness you wear will be detected.

We are all familiar with a situation where a pun is made

during an atmosphere of misery. For a moment, there might be laughter, but the misery is never far behind. True, lasting feelings of joy can only be engendered in response to genuine, heart-felt love, for then there is no veneer to see through. Then love always brings joy – even during miserable circumstances.

Think back to a time when you have been in physical pain – not much to laugh at? Now try and recollect if a nurse or somebody else who genuinely cared for you cracked a joke – even about your condition – and made you laugh. Does it not seem strange to you that you were able to experience feelings of joy through the pain? Yet if that same person had not displayed feelings of concern for you and cracked the same joke, what then?

Even more strange then that you are probably unable to remember the joke which was made with insincerity during a time of misery, yet you are likely to remember precisely what made you laugh when the joy you felt came as a direct result of loving care – there is a sort of permanence about it.

You have been brought your dream for a specific purpose. Whether you have the opportunity to bring joy into somebody else's life, or are being told by your subconscious that you need to experience this healing emotion yourself, there is a valid reason for this message – think about it!

K
KARMA

Were you eating a kebab in your dream, or watching kangaroos cavorting? Or maybe you dreamt of looking at a kaleidoscope of colours, or a regiment of soldiers clad in khaki. Even if your dream simply featured the letter "K" etched in an ornate glass, your subconscious wants you to consider the implications of karma.

We are all familiar with the sayings, "What goes around, comes around" and, "We reap what we have sewn" – essentially this is karma. It is quite uncanny how these sayings often seem to hold true. There are many instances in life when people appear to get what is coming to them: "poetic justice", or "their just desserts".

If you have been suffering patiently in silence at the hands of somebody who has been getting away with injustice for too long, your dream is telling you to hang on a little longer, because the wheel of karma is about to turn full circle on him or her.

However, if it is you who have been getting away with it for too long, this dream is serving as a final warning! Mend your ways now before it is too late. Starting from this moment, take positive action that will lead to the avoidance of the poetic justice which might be waiting for you round the next corner!

But that is just one small aspect of karmic law. If you cannot relate to the above examples, then the message behind your dream might be asking you to consider certain aspects of your life much more deeply than you have before.

If you seem to have been suffering in a rut for a long time, consider why. Ask yourself if these circumstances are of your own making. If it transpires that you have brought about your fate by your own hand, then your subconscious is urging you to find a way out, also by your own hand. Look within yourself and a solution will be found.

On the other hand, if your long-standing problem has not been your responsibility, and you have been bearing the burden as best you can, then take heart. The tide is about to turn, and the positive aspects of karma are soon going to bring rewards and lead to the alleviation of the problem.

The law of karma can have its effects both in the short-term and the long-term. The short-term effects can be almost instantaneous. Something might happen which, at the time, might appear nothing short of a disaster. Then a few moments later an opposite effect takes place which puts everything right and cancels out the consequences of that calamity.

For example, consider a gambler who, after losing everything, is returning home a broken individual, intending to commit suicide. Upon opening the front door, he receives news of a win on the Premium Bonds. A vivid case scenario, but one which illustrates the point – these things do happen.

If then, there are analogous circumstances in your life at this time, and your dream has led you to this page, don't be too hasty in trying to end your problems illogically. Your subconscious is telling you to hold fire for a while, a solution is just around the corner. However, your dream is also warning you to learn a lesson. Perhaps next time an answer might not be so easily forthcoming.

If you are spiritually minded and cannot equate with any of the above examples, then your subconscious is urging you to consider another possible consequence of karmic law, and perhaps the longest-term of all – reincarnation!

Buddhists, among others, hold that the way in which we conduct our lives during this earthly existence will have a direct bearing on our plight in the next incarnation. For example, if you were to spend this life in the pursuit of wealth to the detriment of those who are less fortunate, you might find yourself being born into inescapable poverty in the next incarnation.

Moreover, if you have found this existence to be less than savoury – for whatever reason – and life just does not seem to be fair, consider the question of karma. Could your plight be directly attributable to your actions in your previous existence? Perhaps you are paying off a karmic debt? If this possibility rings a bell, then take heart. Your dream is giving you strength to endure, because the ultimate rewards will far outweigh your present suffering.

Whatever the reason your subconscious brought you to the letter "K", you are being urged to contemplate certain issues in your life. Remember that according to the laws of karma, what you give out, you will ultimately get back. As you judge others, eventually, you will be judged in turn. Therefore, be careful that you treat other people in a manner that you would find acceptable yourself.

L
LUST

Did a lifeboat, a lemur or a lion control the events of your dream? Or perhaps it centred around lilac, legs, land or even limbo dancers? The fact that you have decided to turn to this page indicates that you feel fairly certain your dream highlighted the letter "L" more than any other.

The word lust is usually associated with a passion for sex, so before we take a look at other possible connotations, let us consider why your dream might be alerting you to the subject of sexual lust.

Perhaps you are in an established relationship and have been tempted by forbidden fruits elsewhere? Maybe the opportunity exists for you to give in to the powerful drive of lust? If you are able to identify with this description, your subconscious is alerting you to the possible consequences if you succumbed to this temptation.

Ask yourself whether the short-lived excitement of a brief sexual encounter is worth risking everything. Think of the hurt a selfish act like that could cause to those who are close to you. Unfortunately, nowadays, the divorce courts in the Western hemisphere are full to overflowing with distraught partners who refused to listen to their conscience.

If, on the other hand, you have recently found yourself being the object of somebody else's desire, your subconscious is pointing out that it is a mistake to confuse lust for love. Your dream's purpose is to urge you to think things through before you make a decision.

Perhaps sexual lust does not feature in your life at the moment. Could, then, your subconscious be alerting you to somebody close who, driven by lust, could be about to make a mistake? If you recognize these circumstances, then your dream is asking you to consider whether you could prevent a disaster before it happens.

But lust does not necessarily have to be associated with sex. Indeed, lust could apply to any yearning where the need to have is driven by passionate desire. Lust for riches might be overwhelming, invoking just such desire. In this sense, lust can be one of the most powerful driving forces of humanity, and should be understood. Perhaps it is no mistake that it is listed as one of the original seven deadly sins.

No matter if you are unable to identify with the above examples, your subconscious has brought you the "L" for a reason. There are now, or will be in the near future, circumstances which are likely to be attributed to lust in one form or another. You will be better able to deal with whatever has or is likely to arise if you set aside emotion and view things dispassionately. And that is the message behind your dream.

M
MEDITATION

Predominant dream images of the moon, Merlin, medals, matches, mice, melons or mountains, for example, all indicate that the letter "M" features strongly enough for you to turn to this page and consider the question of meditation.

In the West there are various notions as to what exactly meditation means. Some will hold that it is deep thought centred round religion. Others believe that it is achieving a blank state of mind, while some insist that it represents a state of focused concentration closely allied to deep hypnosis. For the purpose of *The Dream Oracle* we are happy to go along with whatever definition you give to the word meditation, as long as it involves some sort of deep thinking.

To be brought to this page means that your subconscious has identified a need for you to meditate. Perhaps you have been in two minds whether to take up some form of meditation, and have either been too busy, or dismissed the idea for now, setting it aside for another time? If you can identify with this description, your subconscious is urging you to pursue your original idea and learn how to meditate.

There are many benefits to be had in whatever form of meditation you decide to practise – whether it be deep thinking or something more.

Sometimes snap decisions are needed, when only a limited amount of time is available for deep thought. If you are well versed in the mental disciplines of meditation, then even these rapid thoughts may be given more clarity. There is therefore every reason to learn how to focus thoughts more efficiently.

Perhaps, on occasion, you are prone to speaking out without thinking? Maybe your subconscious has identified a need where meditation would benefit and lead to a more balanced approach to life.

Today, there are very few places left on the globe where civilization has not been dragged along by the ever-increasing drive for speed and efficiency. Perhaps it is time for you to slow down, change your mind-set, and consider things more carefully.

There is much evidence to show that good health can be promoted by meditation. Stress-related diseases are among the biggest killers in the world today. If you suspect that you have been driving yourself too hard, your subconscious has brought you this dream with a warning and a message: "Slow down and think things through!"

Perhaps you have been presented with a contract or an opportunity which requires you to make a big decision. If this rings a bell, then your dream is cautioning you to look deeper. On the surface, things might appear to be too good to be true, and, at first glance, you cannot see how anything could go wrong. But ask yourself if you have overlooked some small detail which could have far-reaching consequences and possibly harbour a detrimental outcome.

Conversely, you may be faced with an opportunity which, on the surface, seems inadequate in terms of benefit for you. If this is familiar, look again, delve deeper, and give the issue a lot more thought before dismissing it out of hand. Many times people have imagined that others were trying to exploit them, only to discover, subsequently, that they may have turned their back on what could have been the opportunity of a lifetime.

If you are caught up in a family upheaval, where feelings are running high and there seems to be no solution, then your subconscious is alerting you to the fact that, through meditating on the problem, you will find a compromise acceptable to all parties concerned.

No matter what reason your subconscious has brought you to this section of the book, your dream is stressing that you need to employ some sort of meditation. So start by thinking deeply about what situation your subconscious has identified which could benefit by giving the matter a lot more careful consideration than you would normally apply to such things, and the answer will be revealed.

N
NATURE

Perhaps your dream was dominated by Napoleon, a naval battle, needles, neon signs, Normans, or a nursery; or you might have dreamt of certain aspects of nature itself. Then it is no mistake that you have turned to the letter "N".

Nature is a huge topic, encompassing everything. All that we see, hear and experience has grown out of nature. For the purpose of *The Dream Oracle*, we use a conventional interpretation of the subject. Your dream is linked to the growing, living planet and the creatures who dwell on it, or to the natural aspects of personality. Your subconscious has identified one of these issues which relates to your situation in life, and perhaps to those who surround you.

If you have been in two minds whether to take some sort of positive action to assist nature, for example, by planting a tree, lobbying your political representative, using your car less, or simply allowing your garden to revert to its natural form to encourage the population of butterflies, then your dream is telling you that now is the time to make a start.

On the other hand, through various circumstances, you might be oblivious to the finer aspects of nature. If this description sounds familiar, then your subconscious is urging you to take an interest. Ask yourself if you have ever noticed the beauty and wondrous nature of the simplest of blooms, or even of a blade of grass? Consider the exquisite beauty held within a single raindrop caught in a ray of sunlight, or in the formation of a cloud. Wonder about the longevity of trees, and what plight has befallen the planet during their long lifespan.

Contemplate that our planet exists in a most delicate and finely balanced biosphere, in which all things are interdependent. Despite advances in science, nobody knows the long-term consequences of the tiniest creature becoming extinct, let alone of more seemingly important species higher up in the food chain.

Perhaps you are facing a situation where you are anxious and more than a little unsure of how you should present yourself: a job interview, a public engagement, or an important meeting, for example. If this rings a bell, then your subconscious is telling you to be your natural self.

Many opportunities are missed when people are preoccupied with presenting an image of themselves they consider others might expect. Rarely are these façades convincing, and often they are transparent. You can probably remember somebody being viewed with suspicion because they were presenting themselves falsely.

If people cannot accept you as you are, it is their problem, not yours. Ultimately, other individuals will be able to relate to the real you far better than to a plastic imitation. Barriers begin to tumble and a more relaxed atmosphere usually ensues.

You may suspect that somebody is being less than honest with you, or holding something back. If this sounds familiar, your subconscious is asking you to understand that this person might be presenting an image they think you will find acceptable.

You are likely to discover the truth if you put this person at his or her ease, and encourage the natural, real individual to reveal him- or herself.

Whatever circumstances surround your life at the moment, know that your subconscious has identified a way in which you can improve your existence by becoming more aware of nature, or, perhaps, by identifying the more positive attributes of natural behaviour.

O
OVERUSE

Whether oranges, opals, the opera, an orchestra, olives, ostriches or an orchid predominated in your dream, you have been led to the letter "O", and are urged to consider why your attention has been drawn to the subject of overuse.

To begin with, have you been using *The Dream Oracle* too much lately? That there is a wealth of knowledge and insight to be gleaned from your dreams cannot be denied, but to place too much reliance on them can prove counter-productive.

The secret lies in striking the right balance. Whether we exist in a universe of the mind and all else is an elaborate illusion, or not, consider just how convincing the "illusion" of physical existence is. Even the most dedicated student of the mind has to eat and perform certain physical functions if they wish to survive in this realm of existence.

The fact that you use *The Dream Oracle* demonstrates that you have an extra dimension to your understanding of the universe. However, as with everything else, it is possible to have too much of a good thing.

It is feasible, under certain circumstances, that your subconscious might want you to consider many different aspects of your life. The fact that *The Dream Oracle* allows for direct communication between the subconscious and conscious mind might in itself promote a flood of dreams. Indeed it is likely that you could incubate or receive lots of dreams when you first start to use this book. However, things are likely to settle down soon.

Better that you give the message each dream brings careful consideration over a period of days rather than just a few minutes. Learn to use *The Dream Oracle* with care and respect. Look deep enough to recognize the circumstances to which your dream is alerting you. And learn to meditate on these same issues until a solution reveals itself.

It will be then that you will gain the full benefit and potential of this new system of divination. Using *The Dream Oracle* is exciting, but be patient. Your subconscious is urging this, too, which is why the "O" featured so strongly in your dream.

If you have not been over-indulging yourself in use of *The Dream Oracle*, then your subconscious has identified other circumstances where you have been overusing something else. Overuse of many things can have a detrimental effect, even of those things we think are good for us.

Perhaps you have been jogging too much, or working out in the gym to excess? If you can identify with the overuse of your body in this sort of way, then your dream is cautioning you to ease up a little. The number of things open to abuse through overuse are legion: cramming for exams, too much television, detailed work which puts a strain on the eyes, eating, smoking or drinking in excess.

One thing is for sure, if you have not been using *The Dream Oracle* too much, then your subconscious has identified something in your life to which the message of overuse applies. Your dream is asking you to recognize this problem and take appropriate action.

P
PATIENCE

Perhaps your dream featured things in pairs, maybe there were constant images of paper, pastry, pearls, penguins and pottery, or the events of your dream concerned different aspects of a park. You have obviously decided that the letter "P" was most prevalent, so you have turned to the page concerning patience.

Before patience as a virtue is considered, let us look at the other side of the coin. There are occasions when patience has been stretched to the limit, or when people may take advantage of your patience. Perhaps you have been enduring an almost intolerable situation for too long? If you can identify with circumstances in your life where, deep down, you know you have been too patient, then your subconscious is indicating that the time has come to seek a solution.

This does not necessarily mean you must throw your patient demeanour out of the window. On the contrary, it is because of your capacity to bide your time that your dream is bringing you this message. Use your talent for patience to bring about a satisfactory conclusion. Bide your time and think of a way in which the virtue of patience can work for you. If you spend some time thinking things through, the answer will surface.

Have you been waiting for an advancement in your life – a promotion at work, perhaps? Have others been promoted over your head, so that you now feel put upon, in a rut? Could the reason for this be that others have taken your patient character for granted, and decided that you wouldn't mind waiting a bit longer?

If this sounds familiar, your subconscious is urging you to use your patience to your advantage. Perhaps you should use your time to secure another position which offers better pay and conditions. If nothing presents itself immediately, your capacity for patience will enable you to deal with it. If, on the other hand, you do secure such a position, all to the good. Whatever the outcome, your gift for patience can be turned to your advantage.

For many of us patience is an important virtue we need to acquire. Bear in mind that things usually happen in their own sweet time. Exam results, for example, are usually issued on a predetermined date. Once the rigours of sitting that exam have been endured, there is nothing one can do to alter the outcome. Worrying will not affect the results in the slightest.

Perhaps your patience is being put to the test? Babies and young children often have a talent for pushing patience to the limit. If this sounds familiar, your dream is asking you to strengthen your resolve by changing your mind-set, so that you will be able to cope. Where children are concerned, remember if you allow them to push you over the top, then they have won!

Often when people try to hurry things along or cut corners, details are overlooked or remain unchecked, sometimes with disastrous consequences. This can lead to something having to be redone – sometimes an entire project must be scrapped and started again. There is nearly always a cost, be it financial, physical, spiritual or one of time. A few minutes of patient observation could save a lifetime's regret!

If this description rings a bell, the message is clear: be patient! Perhaps an old Maltese proverb sums it up: "Time gives good advice."

Even if none of these examples seems appropriate to your circumstances, your subconscious has led you to this section of the book for a purpose. Give the issue of patience much thought and you will find the answer.

Q
QUEST

Maybe the most dominant feature of your dream was people quarrelling, or a vision of someone in plain Quaker dress. Dreams of quicksand, a queen, a quadrangle, a barber's shop quartet, or even a quintet, indicate by emphasizing the letter "Q" that these symbols are linked to the subject of a quest.

Maybe you are considering embarking on a journey to find an answer to a problem, or to meet someone who will provide a missing piece to one of life's jig-saws. Perchance it has something to do with your family or career. You could possibly be pursuing a hobby that requires a certain amount of research. If you are able to equate with these examples, then your subconscious is urging you to steel yourself and take the plunge, because you are likely to benefit from the experience.

If, however, embarking on this quest is likely to hurt someone, your dream is telling you to consider the feelings of others. For instance, if your quest would mean leaving behind a loved one who is likely to be stressed by your absence, then the message behind the dream is to employ patience, and consider other possibilities. Ask yourself if your goal can be achieved by different means, such as writing letters.

There are, however, many forms of quest which do not involve a physical journey. If you have been contemplating a quest for academic knowledge and through a lack of self-confidence consider you are deficient in ability, think again! It is no mistake that your dream featured the letter "Q".

Fortunately, your subconscious is not bound by the constraints of low self-esteem. Under these circumstances, the message behind the dream is clear – sign up for evening classes, become a mature student, apply to the university, enrol on the course, or simply take the time to read the books – you can do it!

Perhaps you are just starting a new career and have ambitions of becoming chairman of the board. In that case, your subconscious is indicating that you do indeed have that potential. However, to succeed in such a quest, you need to set out a fairly flexible, medium- to long-term game plan which allows for all foreseen eventualities.

After that, you will have to see it through. Always bear in mind that your subconscious has recognized that you possess the potential to rise to the top of your chosen profession. Therefore, work hard and stick to your strategy. If, in the end, through circumstances beyond your control, you do not secure the top position, you can be sure you will be up there somewhere fairly close.

Bear in mind, however, that ruthless business people will always confirm – if they are honest – that in one form or another, their success has come at a high price. Achieve your goals through your own hard-working, honest endeavours.

Perhaps you have been considering embarking on a spiritual quest. Many people who are not particularly religious in the conventional sense speculate about matters of spirituality, regardless of what beliefs have featured in their upbringing.

Sometimes what they have been taught does not seem to fit into their scheme of things. Perhaps their parents' theology appeared to be too strict, or even too fantastic to accept. These same people can find themselves turned off religion. Nevertheless, a sort of awareness, or consciousness of spiritual being, is never far from their deliberations. But they evidently yearn for something other than the orthodox teachings of various denominations. It is as if they know that there is more to life than merely existing in the physical world, yet they are unable to put a finger on exactly what it is they are seeking.

If this description seems to fit broadly with your own circumstances, then you are meant to read these words. Remember, the first time you scanned this book, your subconscious took it all in. Your dream is telling you it is time to begin your spiritual quest.

It is not the purpose of *The Dream Oracle* to guide you on a specific spiritual course; your subconscious already knows which path you should tread. Putting faith in your intuition is an excellent way to start. Listen to your conscience and allow it to steer you safely on your spiritual search.

If none of the above seems to fit your situation, bear in mind that it was no mistake your dream brought you to this section of the book. Take some time for deep thought as to the reason why, and the way forward will begin to appear. Somehow a quest is relevant to you, or soon will be.

R
REPENTANCE

Whether you dreamed of rust, a reservoir, a record, a rattlesnake, a collection of rugs, or an open razor, if the letter "R" was the most prominent feature of your dream, then you are reading the correct page. Your dream is urging you to consider one of the many aspects of repentance.

Perhaps you have been wronged by somebody who seems oblivious to the fact that you are upset. Maybe you have been erroneously charged with some misdeed and your accuser is ignorant that you are blameless. If these, or similar occurrences apply to you, your dream is advising patience. Don't be too hasty to point out the wrongdoing or to assert your innocence.

Often, when we react to an injustice, we damage our own case by being too obdurate in our attempts to ensure that things are put right, and the truth is established. Therefore, your subconscious is telling you to count to ten, metaphorically, and allow an opportunity for the cause of the injustice to be revealed in due course, or time for you to gather your thoughts and put forward a measured response – one which is likely to establish the facts without inviting scorn or ridicule.

Perhaps your feelings are running high, your pain is deep, and your anger will not allow you to accept a sincere apology. If this sounds familiar, you are being urged to reflect and ask yourself if you have ever committed a similar injury and sought forgiveness. Recall how negative the emotion of anger is, and realize that it can only do harm, that seldom does anything good come from it. Remember what it was like to have your own apology thrown back in your face.

Perhaps, for some years, your conscience has been troubling you over wrongs you committed in the past. Maybe your chance to make amends has long since disappeared with the passage of time, or the death of an old friend or neighbour. If you can relate to these or similar events, then your dream brings a message of forgiveness.

Find solace in the fact that your conscience has troubled you deeply enough to bring you this dream of reassurance and remission. It is precisely because you have been disquieted by your own guilt that you are absolved. Half the battle was won when you admitted the guilt to yourself. The other half was much harder to win, through your continued feelings of remorse. If you had the opportunity now, you would make amends. The heart that is truly sorry deserves forgiveness.

Your subconscious has acknowledged your inner turmoil and suffering, and is now telling you that it is time to let go of the pain – you are forgiven. Now you must learn to heal that wound by learning to love yourself. But before you are able to do so, you must accept this message from your subconscious and learn to forgive yourself. Look forward in confidence, knowing that you have learned your lesson.

Perhaps you have transgressed more recently, and have not yet expressed regret. It is never too late to offer sincere apologies. If true repentance comes from your heart and is not accepted, then any remaining trouble does not rest on your shoulders. If a person apologizes a thousand times without sincerity, each apology is worthless, but one from the heart demands acceptance.

Be aware that pride often prevents us from saying sorry, but know that it is a fool's pride. Recall how many times others have allowed their pride to prevent them from apologizing to you, and recall too what your thoughts were at the time. Truly, to err is human, to forgive, divine.

Repentance is a far-reaching subject encompassing many points worth pondering. Therefore, if none of the above examples seems to apply to you, do not be too surprised. Your subconscious ensured that the letter "R" was predominant within your dream, and is therefore urging you to come up with the solution, because deep down, you know what it is.

S
SLOTH

Maybe your dream brought you visions of a sarcophagus, of strings of sausages, scallops, or scissors. Maybe it was something more striking like a scorpion or an image of Scrooge, or perhaps "S" was the prominent feature in the text on a book cover. If "S" featured vividly in your dream, there are many angles on the subject of sloth to be considered.

Has somebody close to you been displaying symptoms of sloth? Have you found yourself losing patience with this person? Possibly you are contemplating presenting the individual with a kind of ultimatum? Or perhaps you think that a number of people just haven't been pulling their weight, and seem to be getting increasingly lazy?

If these descriptions strike a chord, it was not by chance that your dream was filled with symbols which led you to this page. But consider a few aspects before you take any action.

Deliberate a little on whether the person's behaviour is typical, or could it have been a relatively recent development? Perhaps there is a medical condition causing fatigue, of which the individual is unaware. Sometimes symptoms of depression manifest themselves through seemingly lazy behaviour: a desire to stay in bed, continual tiredness, or a generally apathetic demeanour, to name just three. These symptoms can go unnoticed by those closest to the sufferer, so if these descriptions sound familiar, consider seeking a second opinion and professional help.

Conversely, if you are sure that the reason for this conduct is nothing other than sloth, then your subconscious is urging you to take some action. Teenagers often reach a stage where they appear unwilling to lend a hand around the house. Perhaps your spouse, or somebody close to you, is relying on you most of the time to tidy up after them. It could be a colleague at work, who is content to let you do all the hard tasks, then happily joins the team to share in the credit.

If these, or similar circumstances, ring a bell, your dream is reminding you that sometimes the best remedy for this problem is to mimic the slothful behaviour. Leave the teenagers to wash their own clothes, let your spouse see how the dirty dishes are piling up, and for a change, make yourself scarce at work when the hard slog is due to be done. If the message does not sink in, repeat the medication as often as necessary.

If, however, you have tried these methods and they have failed, then your subconscious has brought you this dream because an opportunity has, or is about to, present itself, which is likely to lead to a solution. Give the matter some thought and you will come up with the answer.

The other side of the coin presents itself if you are aware of becoming sloth-like yourself. Again, ask yourself if this sort of attitude is typical of you. If the answer is no, investigate the possible causes. Have a medical examination, ponder reasons why you might be suffering from some form of depression. If necessary, seek help.

Sometimes slothful behaviour can creep up on us unnoticed – a sort of gradual winding-down. If people have been remarking recently about your lazy ways, then this dream comes to alert you that you are slipping into sloth. You have been led to this page before things get out of hand. If appropriate, seek help; otherwise, change your mind-set and start thinking positively.

On occasion, sloth can be associated with weight problems. If you have recently been gaining weight for no other reason than an unhealthy diet or lack of exercise, then your dream is alerting you to the fact that, apart from medical implications, there are other disadvantages to your current lifestyle.

There are many messages that could be implicit in your dreams about sloth, so if none of these examples seems appropriate to your situation, give the matter some thought and the reason for your dream will be revealed.

T
TALENT

If you dreamed predominantly of trees, trolls, tinsel, teeth, trains, tambourines, or even trifle, then your subconscious has been cueing you to awaken and turn to this page, to reflect on why the subject of talent should have been brought to your attention by your dream.

We all possess a talent which incorporates a facet peculiar to ourselves. Some of us may be gifted in composing music, or in painting, writing, or sculpture; while others might be adept at more obscure skills: meditation, mental arithmetic, gauging the distance of a far-away object, or simply being able to entertain others in some way.

If you are aware of your talent and have been considering developing its potential to make money, help others, or just as a hobby, your dream is indicating that the time is right to begin work. Your subconscious is in accord with your desires and will facilitate your ability to concentrate on honing your skill.

Do not underestimate your worth or that of your talent. If, in the past, for fear of ridicule, you have dismissed the idea of putting your gift to profitable use, your subconscious is telling you to believe in yourself. This may represent the opportunity you have been waiting for, therefore follow your inner urge, and go for it!

Perhaps you are already putting your talent to good use, and have been considering broadening your skills, but are not sure how to go about it? Then your subconscious may be advising you to hold back from looking for a completely different venture. The answer could lie closer to home, and be allied to your existing talent.

Often, by building on existing foundations and elaborating, we are able to break into a whole new world of opportunity. For example, an artist may have been producing fine work which has been admired by friends and relatives for years. Then he or she might evolve a new technique for bringing characters to life on canvas. This could lead to this individual being catapulted to professional status. The late British puppeteer Harry Corbett began by entertaining children with a magic act. He built on that accomplishment by adding and incorporating the puppet Sooty. Fifty years on, his son sold the world rights to Sooty for a seven-figure sum.

If you have been trying to make your talent the vehicle to success in a highly competitive field, your subconscious may be reminding you that to gain the edge over your rivals you need to focus your attention and work that bit harder. Look at new ways in which you can improve or develop your aptitude.

Maybe your dream is not alerting you to your own talent. Perhaps you are in a position where you could utilize somebody else's skills. If you have been wrestling with a problem and getting nowhere, your subconscious is counselling you to seek assistance from somebody who is better suited to effect a solution than yourself. You need help, don't be too proud to ask for it! People are often eager to lend a hand for no other reward than that of displaying their own abilities.

Or perhaps you are being reminded that everybody's gift has a unique aspect to it. Could it be that you need to recognize that each human being does indeed possess some talent, no matter how unlikely it might seem? Is this an opportunity for you to recognize that talent and help the individual to develop it? Perhaps this knack for helping others could be your own, hitherto unknown, skill?

Whatever the reason your dream brought you to this page, you are being urged to consider the many varied aspects of talent. Give the subject sufficient thought and the answer will become clear.

u
UNDERSTANDING

Unicorns, umbrellas, umpires, uncles, ukeleles, urns and uniforms may have been predominant in your dream if your subconscious is urging you to turn to the letter "U". You are meant to read the following text on the subject of understanding.

Understanding is one of the most significant topics in *The Dream Oracle*, and should be weighed up very carefully. The consequences of insufficient understanding in life can be dire. Lack of understanding, or unwillingness even to try, are responsible for much that is wrong in the world today.

For instance, if a more sincere effort were made by countries with opposing points of view to understand one another better, perhaps differences could be set aside and a lasting peace forged. First, though, a firm commitment is needed by both sides in a genuine attempt to comprehend each other's point of view. Imagining oneself in somebody else's shoes often results in a hitherto unrecognized revelation. The seeds of understanding are sown and allowed to grow and develop into something approaching empathy.

In fact, most wars, conflicts, arguments and disputes of all types – no matter how large or small – are caused or perpetuated by a lack of understanding. Most man-made problems in the world exist because of humanity's reluctance to try to see things from the other side. Therefore it is vitally important that we begin to grasp the enormous significance and potential of changing our mind-set from that of seeing things mostly from our own perspective to that of making the effort to comprehend others' viewpoints.

If true understanding were given higher priority, perhaps the high incidence of divorce in the West would be greatly reduced. If both parties really attempted to understand each other, many disagreements could be avoided. A little understanding goes a long way.

Perhaps it is not you who lacks understanding, but instead it could be somebody close to you. Ask yourself if you are in a position to enable this person to grasp a different way of thinking. You will have to do so gently if you have taken the time to appreciate his or her stance.

Children, especially, require a lot of understanding. If we simply lay down a set of rules and make no attempt to learn how they affect the young ones, how can we expect them to grow with understanding themselves?

It is no accident that your dream has brought you to this portion of the book, because there is probably a situation in your life that would be best resolved by employing greater perception. Perhaps you are an understanding person by nature? If so, then your subconscious has identified a temporary slip in your usually sympathetic attitude. Look deeper at the other person's motives, and try just that little bit harder to understand.

If, however, you have read this section and admit that you do not generally make as much effort to understand as you should, then your subconscious is urging you to make a start today.

Whatever the reason your dream has brought you to the subject of understanding, it is important that you give this matter some serious consideration. The truth will then be revealed!

V
VANITY

If your dream featured such objects as valves, vandals, velcro, vegetables, villas, vases or even a ventriloquist, and stood out vividly enough for you to consider turning to this page, then your subconscious has some good reason to attract your attention to the subject of vanity.

There are a myriad facets to vanity, which perhaps you have not taken into account before. Vanity is sometimes associated with pride. For instance, if a recent achievement has invoked feelings similar to job satisfaction, then justifiably you may take a certain amount of pride in your work. Under these circumstances, your dream is one which bears a message of reassurance and encouragement. Your subconscious is giving you a pat on the back for a task well done, and urging you to maintain your high standards.

Similarly, perhaps you are proud of your children, a family member, or a friend who has attained worthwhile success. If this description rings a bell, then your dream is suggesting that you let the person concerned know how pleased you are at such an achievement. After all, everyone deserves praise for a job well carried out.

But vanity can also be taken at its face value. At its most negative, vanity can be very destructive, especially to those who are close to you and, ultimately, to yourself as well. We all experience feelings of vanity from time to time, but the secret is to deal with them positively. For example, there is no harm in taking pride in one's personal appearance. It can be reassuring to receive admiring glances, and register them in one's memory. But we are all familiar with the "poseur", who blatantly struts around advertizing the fact that he or she is adorned in the latest, most expensive designer labels, or sports a hairstyle which has cost a fortune. And we are all aware of how these people come across to us. Strangely enough, these same individuals never seem to realize exactly what sort of impression they do create.

The Dream Oracle is not in the business of arguing the merits of capitalism versus communism, or of comparing wealth with poverty. However, if you have turned to this page, your subconscious evidently wishes you to consider certain aspects of vanity.

If you are in the lucky position of being materially better off than the average, you are reminded that it is wise to enjoy your good fortune discreetly. To parade one's wealth publicly with an air of superiority in front of those who are less favoured is tantamount to rubbing their noses in it – which could invite an adverse reaction.

Vanity can also be destructive as we approach middle age. Wrinkles begin to appear, the skin starts to lose its lustre, the hair can turn grey, and our general energy levels slowly decrease.

We now live in an age, particularly in the West, when face-lifts, lipo-suction, hair transplants, wonder lotions and miracle foundation creams are thrust at us. Glossy magazines are just one form of the media to fill their coffers with advertising revenue for these same services and products. The message comes across in a way designed to make us feel like second-rate citizens if we don't at least consider using them.

If you are concerned about your looks as you enter middle age, your dream has brought you to the "V" for a purpose which demands serious attention. These "miracle" products and services cannot stop you from ageing. But the brainwashing razzmatazz which is designed to entrap us in a sort of plastic-skinned political correctness can psychologically prevent us from ageing with dignity if we succumb and join the "in crowd". It is a travesty of human values to prey on the understandable weakness of vanity in this way.

This same indoctrination is targeted to undermine confidence, sow a seed of doubt and, specifically, to appeal to vanity. Paradoxically then, your subconscious is also appealing to your vanity, to help you avoid being sucked into a world of low self-esteem, believing that unless you invest vast quantities of money in a futile attempt to avoid ageing, you are somehow inferior.

The message behind the dream is that you should be proud of the way you are. Believe in yourself, and do not feel that unless you take anti-ageing measures, you are ready for the scrap heap. History is full of accounts of older people who have invited love, respect and success simply by being themselves.

So use vanity in a positive way. Understand that, as you grow older, other attributes will surface, attributes which will be more than a substitute for a youthful physical appearance.

Learn to love yourself, and to be satisfied with the way you look. Believe in yourself and be proud of who you are!

If none of these examples seems to fit the bill and apply to your circumstances, then your subconscious is alerting you to another aspect of vanity. If you give the subject enough thought, the reason for your dream will be clarified.

W
WILL

Dreaming predominantly of wine, wagons, wheels, whales, wheat, whisky, wigs, or whistles is a certain indication that your subconscious has absorbed the following text and, through your dream, is demanding that you turn your attention to the subject of will.

Perhaps you have been striving to achieve an objective, only to find an unforeseen obstacle apparently thwarting your efforts. Under these circumstances, it is easy to give up and allow despair and dejection to take over. "Why should I bother?" is a common response, or, "What has it all been for?"

If this description sounds familiar, then your dream is bringing you an explicit message. Do not give up! In hindsight, many people have realized that, if they had persisted in their attempts for just a bit longer, their goal would have been reached.

Instead of viewing an obstacle as the last straw, give the matter some deep thought. Look for ways in which a disadvantage can be turned to an advantage. Seek a silver lining in the blackest of clouds. Often, the mere fact of employing a positive attitude can enable the problem to be seen in a new, less obstructive light, facilitating the discovery of a solution.

Perhaps you are embarking on a new path in life: a career, hobby, or educational pursuit. If so, your dream is telling you that to win through, you must have the will to stick at it and succeed. Things that are worthwhile in life seldom come easily.

Or maybe you are in disturbing circumstances which are, or threaten to be, long-term. Perhaps you or somebody close to you has been diagnosed with an illness that will require love, understanding and help. Possibly a seemingly insufferable state of affairs has developed in the workplace, such as a new colleague, with whom you feel unable to work, being thrust upon you. This dream is alerting you to any situation where your strength of will is going to be put to the test, and urging you not to give up.

The other side of the coin, however, is when an excess of will and determination can become akin to stubbornness. Perhaps you are in a position where you previously opted to pursue a certain course, come hell or high water. If this sounds familiar, your dream could be asking you to take stock and look at the issues again. Perhaps circumstances have changed in some way, and your drive to succeed is no longer appropriate.

Moreover, people sometimes stridently decide that a particular course of action is thoroughly justified only to realize later that they had misjudged the original situation. Then a thorny choice presents itself either to withdraw, change course and/or apologize. If this description seems applicable, then your subconscious is urging you to swallow your pride and admit your error. Indeed, it is likely is that you have already recognized the necessity to reassess matters but feel that you might lose face.

Consider, then, how owning up to a mistake often displays strength of character rather than weakness. Everybody makes errors of judgement, but it is the person who is willing to acknowledge a blunder who usually gains the respect and understanding of others.

If you are unable to identify with any of the above and hold strong religious beliefs, perhaps your dream has identified the need for you to turn your will over to God. Maybe there is some problem which, after considering all the options, still seems insurmountable. If this strikes a chord, then you are being asked to trust in God to see you through these troubled times. Have faith in your prayers, open your heart and surrender your will to God. He will not let you down, but will guide you to a solution, albeit in a way which, at first, might appear to be unexpected.

Whatever the cause, the fact that your dream prompted you to turn to this section in the book is a clear sign that you should consider the subject of will. If you do so, you should find the reason.

X
X-RAY

Possibly you dreamt of the letter "X" imprinted on a textured surface – a sandy beach, perhaps? Whether you dreamed of being X-rayed in hospital, or operating a xerox machine, being involved in Xmas activities, or playing a tune on a xylophone, your subconscious is alerting you to turn to the subject of X-ray, or more appropriately, the need to see through things, to look deeper than face value.

Perhaps you have encountered somebody recently who seems too good to be true. Often, loneliness or a longing to feel close to somebody can blind us to the real person, or the situation or circumstances surrounding an individual or event. There are occasions when, for fear of losing contact, we don't wish to see the truth, and a degree of denial takes over.

Deep down there are bound to have been warning signs – no matter how slight. If you are able to connect with this description, then your subconscious is warning you that the time has come to take a closer look, accept the truth and, despite the possible weakening of contact, acknowledge that you will be better off in the long run.

Maybe you have been offered the opportunity of a lifetime, or have the chance to purchase something at a price so low it appears too good to turn down. The fact that you have had this dream indicates that you have held off coming to a decision, or you would have already made your choice. Therefore you are being required to examine the reasons why you resolved to sleep on it. Ask yourself if the motive for your delay was that you were somehow suspicious. Then investigate the possible grounds for those suspicions. Certainly you are being advised to act with caution, to be aware of the possible pitfalls as well as the advantages.

Or perhaps you have recently made a decision and have experienced a niggling doubt about it? You are being urged to look deeper into yourself. Search out the real cause for your apprehension. Isolate it and meditate on it. It might transpire that it is not too late to change your mind.

Consider whether even a small loss might be worth bearing, instead of being drawn into a situation where you could be throwing good money after bad, or taking the first step on what could be a slippery slope all the way to despair. If this is the case, then you are being urged to act now before it is too late. Better to face the music at this stage than to bear the full brunt further on.

Or perhaps you are not happy with your physical appearance, in which instance your dream is bringing you a message of reassurance. Next time you look in the mirror, seek beyond the outer aspect, which may be enhanced with cosmetics. Gaze into the reflection of your own eyes and know the real person behind the superficial appearance.

Your subconscious knows that you are truly a beautiful person, worthy of more than pondering on your physical attributes. Shed the doubts you have been harbouring, and realize that looks are not important in the scheme of things.

If the reason for your lack of confidence has been brought about by an insensitive remark or even a rejection from a would-be partner, recognize that it is these individuals who are the short-sighted ones, the ones who cannot see beyond the ends of their own noses. They are the ones who have no real understanding of what comprises true beauty. Throw off your doubts and know that you possess the most important type of beauty that exists – that of the sensitive, loving soul.

This is even more relevant if you believe in life after death, for it has been said that true beauty and true ugliness will then be revealed. Those who make the mistake of prizing physical aspects above all else might well be tainting the true appearance of the soul. Whereas a person who puts the more important qualities in life such as love, kindness and forgiveness above the surface attractions of the material world will, ultimately, be seen in the resplendent glory of the truly beautiful soul.

As with most topics in *The Dream Oracle*, there is another side to the coin. Possibly you have been looking too deeply into something – being too suspicious, trying to find fault for the sake of it, which is a negative activity. If this suggestion strikes something deep inside you, then your subconscious is urging you not to be too cynical. There are occasions when somebody or something is so genuine that it can appear just too good to be true.

From time to time these wonderful things do come our way. It is then that we must learn to trust and simply accept what is available in the spirit in which it is offered, and feel joy at the kindness which invariably lies behind it.

The fact that your dream chose to wake you at a point when the "X" was prominent in your mind is proof that your subconscious needed you to turn to this section in the book in order to consider the advantages or otherwise of looking beneath the surface. If you do so, you will then discover the real reason for your dream.

Y
YESTERDAY

Your dream could have featured a flotilla of yachts, yarn, yarrow, a yashmak or a yak. Perhaps you dreamed of the American Civil War and Yankees were the predominant feature, or maybe somebody yawned continually, or the colour yellow made a powerful impression on you when you awoke. You might have simply seen the letter "Y". If so, your subconscious requires you to study the subject of yesterday.

The word represents the past, and your subconscious has identified a need for you to examine an aspect of your own history, whether it be yesterday or several years ago.

Consider if, recently, you have acted prematurely on some issue, perhaps said something you now regret, or judged somebody before you were aware of all the facts. If you can relate to any of this, your subconscious is pressing you to take courage and make amends. It can sometimes require a great deal of courage to admit an error and apologize. However, the chances are that in the long-run, your honesty will improve your standing with others.

Perhaps you are encountering a situation similar to one which occurred at some point in your past, in which case your dream is impelling you to make comparisons. Stop and contemplate the lessons that were learned from your past experience, and assess how best they could be applied to your current predicament. Maybe you are being cautioned not to make the same mistakes again. On the other hand, your subconscious might be alerting you to a way round a problem by re-creating a state of affairs parallel to the situation in which you currently find yourself today.

Think things through and consider the consequences of that past incident. Recall the sequence of events which ensued as a result. Contemplate the alternatives. If different action had been taken, would it have led to more beneficial developments? Perhaps a valued relationship could have been saved, or a situation salvaged?

There is good reason for you being directed to this section of *The Dream Oracle*, so if at first you are unable to make the connection, think again. Your subconscious knows exactly why and has used this book in order to bring an issue to your conscious attention.

Maybe you have already recognized that your present circumstances seem strangely similar to a past experience. Then your dream could be urging you to remember the lessons which were learnt, so that you do not make the same mistakes all over again.

Perhaps you have been feeling depressed recently. If so, remember that depression can be deepened by negative thought patterns. If this rings a bell with you, then your dream is telling you that it is important for you to change your mind-set or thought patterns. Remember that there have been many good times in the past, and there will be again.

Moreover, your dream is providing you with an excellent place from which to start altering your mind-set. Indeed, it is even showing you how this can be done. Bring to mind the happiest event of recent times that you are able to recollect. Reflect on what made this occasion so joyful. Give the matter a lot of consideration and try to retrieve those same patterns of thought which were present during that happy time. Before long, you will be unable to resist smiling. When you reach that point, build on those thoughts and know that things cannot remain at a low level forever. Your subconscious is firmly declaring that you can bounce back!

On the other hand, there can be a downside to recalling memories of the past. Possibly you have been living in the past too much lately. Sometimes bereavement can keep us tethered in a negative way to yesterday. It is our natural right to grieve for the loss of a loved one – but for how long before we start to pick up the pieces again?

Nobody can put a time limit on grief – it varies from person to person. However, there comes a point when we have to start the process of rebuilding our lives. It is good to remember the loved one, and nobody would suggest otherwise. Nevertheless, consider whether that same loved one would want you to continue grieving to the detriment of all else. Your subconscious is encouraging you to recollect that happy period, recall the amount of drive in your life during those days and retrieve that same feeling of get-up-and-go. You can do it! The time has come to rebuild!

If you are unable to relate to any of the above examples, it should not be too surprising, especially when we realize that the subject of yesterday could encompass literally hundreds of circumstances. However, accept that your subconscious has identified a need for you to ponder this subject. Give it enough thought and the reason for your dream will surface. Always bear in mind the other side of the coin – in other words, avoid dwelling too much in the past.

Z
ZEN

Whether you dreamed of being on the African plains among a herd of zebras, saw a pattern of zig-zags, zips, Zener cards, zeros, the zoo, or simply witnessed a clear representation of the letter "Z", your dream is prompting you to consider the implications of certain aspects of Zen.

It is said that Zen originated from a Japanese sect of Buddhists, who believed that the truth could not be gleaned from any of the scriptures. Instead, they maintained that the truth is held within the heart, and that the only way to discover it is to master the art of deep thought or meditation.

So why has your dream brought you to this section of *The Dream Oracle*? Perhaps you have been denying the existence of your darker side – warts and all! We all have a side to us that, in varying degrees, we would prefer not to acknowledge. Alcohol can bring it to the fore with some, while others can be prompted by a bad mood, envy, lust, pride or impatience, to name but a few such triggers.

It is important that we recognize these failings and strive to maintain some sort of control over their negative effects. It is even better if we get to know these unsavoury character traits and learn how to eradicate them or change them into less destructive forces. If you suspect that your darker side has been adversely affecting your life, then your subconscious is pressing you to look within, to identify these undesirable features, and then make the effort to mend matters.

Whatever the reason for your dream, one thing is clear, the truth that you seek or need to seek is to be found within yourself. Regardless of what problem you are facing, your subconscious is insisting that if you search hard enough, you will find the truth inside you, to help you overcome your difficulty. So resist the temptation to put the onus on somebody else, for the answer lies in you.

Perhaps you have been experiencing a problem in a close relationship with a spouse, family member or a friend? Maybe the situation has developed to such an extent that you are unable to remember how the original dispute grew to fruition and who was responsible – unfortunately, time has a habit of distorting the memory process. If this scenario sounds familiar, your subconscious is prodding you to disregard attempts at deciding who was first at fault. Instead, recognize that you have the capacity to see the real truth, what really matters, and to use that same truth, or inner wisdom, to put things back on an even keel.

Perhaps you are facing the most important decision of your life – the destiny of a loved one, an issue of health, finance, career, or indeed your own fate. Then your dream is bringing you a message of reassurance. Your subconscious knows that if you look within yourself, to the depths of your heart, you will find the courage to make whatever decision is necessary, and be secure in the knowledge that your motives were pure, born from your heart. Remember to temper your choice with level-headed common sense – there is often room for compromise.

If, later, it transpires that you wonder if you have made the wrong choice, spend time thinking through the possible consequences if you had taken the alternative route. Then ask yourself if you could have lived with yourself and been faithful to yourself, had your motives not been true. Know that no blame can be attached to you for seeking the truth, blending it with level-headed thinking and acting on it.

No matter what we do in life, if we can learn to recognize and bring out the truth within, it will shine like a beacon for all to see. Each and every one of us has the ability to transform our lives by finding the truth within.

If none of the above examples seems applicable to you, the fact that your dream has brought you to the subject of Zen is a clear indication that, for whatever reason, your subconscious has identified the need for you to search within your heart to find your own truth.

BIBLIOGRAPHY

Adler, A. (1958) *What Life Should Mean to You*. Capricorn, New York.

Aubrey, J. (1890; orig. 1696) *Miscellanies*. Library of Old Authors, Reeves & Turner, London.

de Becker, R. (1968) *The Understanding of Dreams, or the Machinations of the Night*. George Allen & Unwin, London.

Dement, W. (1972) *Some Must Watch While Some Must Sleep*. Freeman & Co., San Francisco.

Dixon, N. (1960) "Apparent Changes in the Visual Threshold; Central or Peripheral." *British Journal of Psychology*, Vol 51, (4), 297-309.

Dodds, E. (1971) "Supernormal Phenomena in Classical Antiquity." *Proceedings of the Society for Psychical Research*, 55 (205), 189-237.

van Eeden, F. (1913) "A Study of Dreams." *Proceedings of the Society for Psychical Research*, XXVI (part LXVII), 431-461.

Ephron, H. & Carrington, P. (1966) "Rapid Eye Movement Sleep and Cortical Arousal." *Psychological Review*, 73, 500-526.

Evans, C. & Newman, E. (1964) "Dreaming : an Analogy from Computers." *New Scientist*, 24, 577-579.

Freud, S. (1961; orig. 1900) *The Interpretation of Dreams*. George Allen & Unwin, London.

Freud, S. (1966; orig. 1922) *Jokes and their Relation to the Unconscious.* Routledge & Kegan Paul, London.

Gauquelin, M. (1973) *The Cosmic Clocks.* Granada Publishing Ltd., Herts., England.

Green, C. (1968) *Lucid Dreams.* Institute for Psychophysical Research, Oxford.

Hearne, K. (1978) *Lucid Dreams – an Electrophysiological and Psychological Study.* Department of Psychology, University of Liverpool, England.

Hearne, K. (1982) "An Ostensible Precognition of the 1974 Flixborough Disaster." *Journal of the Society for Psychical Research,* 51 (790), 210-213.

Hearne, K. (1986) "An Analysis of Premonitions Deposited Over One Year, From an Apparently Gifted Subject." *Journal of the Society for Psychical Research,* 53 (804), 376-382.

Hearne, K. (1989) *Visions of the Future.* Aquarian Press, Wellingborough, England.

Hearne, K. (1990) *The Dream Machine.* Aquarian Press, Wellingborough, England.

Jung, C. (1964) *Man and his Symbols.* Aldus Books, London.

MacKenzie, N. (1965) *Dreams and Dreaming.* Aldus Books, London.

Melbourne, D. & Hearne, K. (1997) *Dream Interpretation – the Secret.* Blandford Press, London.

Melbourne, D. & Adams, H. (1997) *Your Dreams and Your Stars.* Blandford Press, London.

Ullman, M., Krippner, S., & Vaughan, A. (1970) *Dream Telepathy.* Macmillan, New York.

ACKNOWLEDGEMENTS

The authors would like to acknowledge all the people who have, over the years, sent in accounts of their dreams to us for interpretation. It was the study of their dreams that led to *The Dream Oracle*'s alphabetical meanings. Thanks, too, to Joan Newby for checking the manuscript.

The authors are keen to hear about reader's experiences with the *Dream Oracle*. Please write to us at:

PO Box 5
Lyness
Stromness
Orkney, Scotland
KW16 3NU
UK

The *Dream Oracle* website is at www.dreamthemes.force9.co.uk

INDEX